Information, communication, and the
paperwork explosion

Information, communication, and the paperwork explosion

Trevor J. Bentley

London · New York · St Louis · San Francisco · Auckland
Düsseldorf · Johannesburg · Kuala Lumpur · Mexico · Montreal
New Delhi · Panama · Paris · São Paulo · Singapore · Sydney · Tokyo
Toronto

Published by McGRAW-HILL Book Company (UK) Limited
MAIDENHEAD · BERKSHIRE · ENGLAND

07 084468 2

Library of Congress Cataloging in Publication Data
Bentley, Trevor J
    Information, communication, and the paperwork explosion.
    Bibliography: p.
    Includes index.
    1. Business records.   2. Communication in management.
    I. Title.   II. Title: Paperwork explosion.
HF5736.B38   658.4'53   76-62
ISBN 0-07-084468-2

Printed and bound in Great Britain

To Liz

Contents

Foreword   viii

Acknowledgements   ix

                                                            Page No.

Part 1   The background   1

    1   Paperwork   3
    2   The paperworker   15

Part 2   Controlling paperwork   31

    3   In the beginning   33
    4   The pathfinder   43
    5   Finding a better path   61
    6   Artist at work   71
    7   Introducing change   92

Part 3   Controlling paperworkers   105

    8   The right environment   107
    9   Setting the right example   119
   10   Getting people to talk to each other   126

Appendices   133

    1   Procedure flowcharts   135
    2   Example: data collection   142
    3   Example of analysis and specification   156
    4   Office design and layout   164
    5   Assessing work content   169
    6   Form control   173

Bibliography   180

Index   181

Foreword

Paperwork is considered by many people to be a necessary evil. It is far from this; it is the basis of communication and the general transference of information. There are many other methods of communication, and much of paperwork is being transferred to these new technologies, but paper has not yet given way to any completely satisfactory medium. Its role is not only increasing; it is becoming a problem in very many areas in industry. The aim of this book is to set down principles of systematically analysing paperwork needs and developing the most appropriate and efficient system for dealing with those needs. There is no magic in this: it is basically common sense applied to an area in industry and commerce which has never received the organizational attention that it deserves. The problem will be approached from an understanding of the role of paperwork and the people involved. It will consider in some detail how paperwork can be effectively controlled and how we can ensure that the minimum of effort is applied to an area which is at best considered to be a non-productive necessity.

This book is the outcome of many years of experience in successfully applying the principles and methods set down. The format of the book has been designed to allow a logical development of thought and as a step-by-step working guide. Part 1 deals with the background to the problems of paper, i.e., the nature of paper and the people who use it. Part 2 contains the rules of effectively controlling paperwork by efficient systems design. Part 3 handles the paperwork problems created by people and how these can be overcome. The appendices deal with certain detailed aspects of methods and techniques which will clarify the text.

Application of the points contained in this book will lead to reduced clerical costs and increased effectiveness. It is hoped that the reader will not only make use of the contents, but also enjoy reading the book.

Trevor J. Bentley

ACKNOWLEDGEMENTS

I would like to thank Christine Ayre and George Pickerill for their hard work in reading, correcting and suggesting improvements to the initial draft. My thanks also go to Vincent Healy for his encouragement and to John Warnock for access to his notes on Introducing Change.

My special thanks to Ted Morgan without whose help this book would have been out in 1974.

I am very grateful to Geraldine Dunne and Jean Wayper whose patience and tolerance in reading my terrible handwriting never flagged.

And finally my warmest thanks to Sue Butler for setting out and typing the final draft.

Part 1
The background

1 Paperwork

Paper

Paper has for many years been the means by which information has been communicated to the mass of people. In very early times, before paper was available, other methods were used which had a far more limited circulation due to the costs involved. Nowadays paper is relatively cheap and with modern methods of preparation vast quantities of information can be documented and transmitted throughout the world at extraordinary speeds. This technology has created enormous problems in terms of receiving, reading and using the information transmitted. Increasing size and complexity in industry and commerce have created demands for growing amounts of information, and the trend towards management at a distance creates the need for a good deal of additional transmission of data. It is because of this that we are faced today with the vast numbers of clerical personnel and with the growing importance and size of the information industry. How in the future can we cope with this enormous amount of data, and how is paper to play its part?

It is probable that paper will always be used, it is doubtful whether any other medium will be discovered which is as economic, as effective and as easy to handle. This has been the main problem. Its low cost and ease of handling have tended to increase the amount of paperwork. But paper does not in itself make problems, it is the people who handle, prepare and use it who do so. The paper industry has consumed much of the earth's timber. Millions of trees have had to be felled to satisfy the insatiable demands for paper. How in the future can paper be limited to those areas where it is necessary? Why should paper be used? What are its really dominant characteristics which prevent the development of a satisfactory substitute?

Paper has two distinct advantages, convenience and economy. First, convenience, this takes the form of both the material itself and methods of handling it. Paper is extremely flexible, it can be folded,

3

torn, cut, burnt, shredded, written on, printed on, photocopied, punched, perforated and chemically treated.

If you consider how often you handle paper you will soon realize that paper is not only used for communications, there are many domestic uses, i.e., tissues, paper plates, paper cups, just about paper everything. It is the versatility of paper which gives it its importance. Some of its principal benefits are the ease with which one can print on a sheet of paper and fold it into a convenient size to be despatched, and, of course, paper envelopes are used mainly because they are easy to address and light. Even files for holding papers are made of cardboard, which is made from the same raw material as paper. Although in recent times plastic has become increasingly used, paper still remains the dominant means of both preparing office communications and of storage.

The second reason for the wide use of paper is its economy. The economy of paper is undoubted. Thousands of sheets of paper can be bought for a few pounds, it isn't the cost of paper itself which makes paperwork so expensive, it is the work which is done to make the paper a means of communication. Paper in most of its forms is comparatively cheap, and people who try to save paper, unless it is in vast quantities, are aiming at a pretty purposeless approach to reducing paperwork. The cost of paper is such that even large savings in volume are small in value and it is, therefore, the work which people do with paper which must merit attention.

One of the major problems of using something which is relatively cheap is that there is no cost basis for limiting its use. Over the years this has created a tremendous surplus of paper flowing through most systems and procedures. The low costs makes people feel that extra copies are not burdening the company with significant expenditure.

The fallacy in this is that an extra copy from a two-part document increases the cost proportionally. In addition to the volume consideration a more insidious and less-appreciated cost is incurred. The extra copies have to be handled in the system, and it is this handling which is so expensive. In this sense the very economy of paper, which results in its excessive use, is creating many of the problems we find in industry and commerce.

However, paper is for the foreseeable future going to be used as the basis of information systems and procedures. The development of sophisticated computing techniques in the future may well alter this situation, but there is a long way to go before facilities are available for the automatic input and output services which would obviate the need for paper. In addition, it is going to be difficult to persuade business people that paper is not necessary as a means of confirming or of 'putting in writing' verbal communication. It is only recently that the courts have begun to accept microfilm copies of original documents. Important documents, such as contracts, deeds, etc., are still required to be in writing, and on high quality paper.

The physical properties and uses of paper have been very carefully analysed over the years and are now fully recognized, and a lot of sophisticated equipment has been developed for its printing and preparation. These developments go all the way through the various processes right up to the shredding or burning at the destruction end of the scale. Paper therefore has become almost an end in itself. Equipment and procedures have been developed to a stage where it would be extremely expensive if the use of paper were to be abandoned for some new product.

With the developments in paper technology, it has been increasingly possible to create more paper with greater ease. No Carbon Required (NCR) paper increases the number of copies which can easily be made at one writing. Even carbon paper, which had its problems, increased the amount of paper used, but NCR paper, being much cleaner and much easier to use, is doing so to an even greater extent.

One paper company has developed a marketing strategy to persuade businessses to change to the use of NCR, the aim being that the more NCR is used, the more paper they will sell, therefore the more profitable will be their business. It is these kinds of pressures which cause the use of paper to escalate, even in the light of improving technology and the development of other media. Paperworkers have to resist all these pressures and to do so is not easy. It requires a type of person who is able to look logically and analytically at all the problems associated with the use of paper. The aim of this book is to make people think, to make them think about paper, about the processes through which it goes and the use that is made of it in industry and commerce. Only a deeper understanding of paper in this context can lead to the effective control of paperwork.

The home of paperwork

The office is the central point in an organization for controlling the paperwork procedures and systems. There may be more than one office in an organization, but most have a head office. Why is work organized in such a way that offices are necessary? In general terms, the role of the office in the organization is, first, as a centre of communication, second, a means of coordination, third, a place for the maintenance of records, and fourth, for the processing of data. Figure 1.1 shows the office represented as the hub of a wheel, the spokes represent communications and the rim represents the operations. The analogy is that the hub is the driving force, the spokes the means of transmitting this force to the rim where the work is done.

To establish the need for an office, it is necessary to look a little closer at what the office does for the organization. This must be dealt with in very general terms, as many offices deal with different parts of procedures and systems in different organizations. Nevertheless, most of the offices are in existence solely to handle paperwork in order to achieve the four main functions listed above. Paperwork is not only done in the office. The office really handles paperwork which is created to a large extent outside the office, in departments such as production, sales, etc. Similarly, clerical activi-

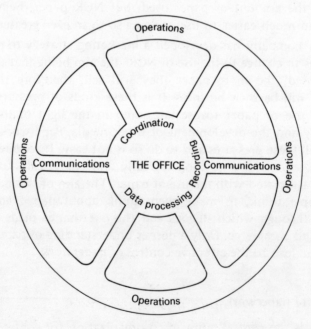

Fig. 1.1

ties are not the prerogative of the office. The majority of people employed in industry and commerce have to do some clerical work, even if it is only filling in a time sheet and using clock cards. Various production documents have to be completed and when one examines paper flowing through an organization it becomes obvious that the majority of it has been created by people whose clerical ability cannot be rated very highly. Of course, they are not employed primarily to do clerical work, and clerical work is considered by them as a nuisance and as a task to be dealt with as quickly as possible or in many cases to be avoided altogether.

But back to the office. The office is organized in such a way as to provide the most appropriate means of handling data, the majority of which is on paper. Offices are often subdivided into specialist functions, such as the accounts department, the sales department, wages department, distribution department, etc.

All these departments have one prime role, the handling of information; its collection, processing and dissemination. These three activities must be carried out if the office is to achieve its roles of communication, coordination, recording and processing. It can be likened to an information factory which collects raw data from a variety of sources. It feeds this raw data into a variety of production processes incorporating many sophisticated machines and finally produces the finished product of information. However, unlike a factory which produces goods according to demand, the office produces information almost at will, frequently not on demand, but because the production processes can easily produce that information. Whether or not it is needed is another matter altogether, and not one that is often examined in any depth. The blame for this particular problem does not lie entirely with the office managers, for it is clearly the responsibility of management to identify their information needs and for the office to satisfy them as efficiently as possible. However, office managers cannot be totally absolved from blame as it is they who create an aura of mystery once the processing of data commences. With the introduction of sophisticated computers, this mystery has grown still deeper and now borders on magic. But there is nothing innately magical in how data is processed, the operations are basically very simple, it is the volume, speed and the complexity of organizing these operations which creates the air of mystery. The processes themselves are very simple. The office has been blamed for the creation of a great deal of surplus paperwork, but as will be seen later it is not only the office which is to blame, but also those whom it serves.

Communication

As a centre of communication the office is becoming essential to the organization. In the office are housed the telephone exchange, the telex machine, the telecopier, and computer terminals. Most communications go through the office. If the office does not receive information which is relevant, it is quite possible that it will produce incorrect documentation. This, in its turn, can have detrimental effects throughout the whole organization, particularly in the sphere of customer relations.

> A salesman visiting his customer was aked to amend the order placed the previous week to read three red and three yellow. The salesman agreed to this and said that he felt that at this stage of production it was quite possible that this could be done at no extra cost. He contacted the sales office and informed them that the customer required to amend the order. The office created the appropriate amendment form and passed it to the production control department. The production control department referred to their previously issued job sheet in order to put the amendment into effect, and, in so doing, they found it was marked 'cancelled', and took no further action. Two weeks later six yellow items were delivered to the customer who naturally complained to the salesman that the order had not been properly executed. Three were returned to be resprayed red. The work was carried out and the goods were despatched one week later to the customer together with an invoice for the additional cost of spraying. This created a further complaint from the customer which, when eventually sorted out by the salesman, necessitated the issuing of a credit note. During the whole process much ill will was created. If only the production control had checked whether the order had or had not been cancelled in the light of the further instruction to amend the colours, the subsequent problems could probably have been avoided. But there had been a simple lack of communication.

Poor communications are a major problem, and if the office handles this part of its procedures efficiently many pieces of paper will never see the light of day.

Coordination

Coordination is also a role which the office attempts to carry out. Its attempts are not often successful. Coordination means the bringing together of people with common interests so that their combined

Fig. 1.2   Coordination

efforts will be pointed in the same direction. All too frequently people with the best will in the world working hard and apparently efficiently do so pulling in opposite directions. The problem has been spotted by the donkeys in the cartoon. They have also found a solution.

A medium-sized engineering company had a coordination problem in the buying and stocking of manufactured parts. The stores controller was trying to keep the stock level as low as possible and yet provide an efficient service to the production department. The production manager was concerned that whenever parts were needed they should be available. Obviously to suit one it would have been necessary to have very low minimum stocks, and to suit the other very high minimum stocks. Replenishment of stocks was carried out by the stores controller using a purchase requisition procedure which indicated to the buyer parts and quantities required to maintain the stock level. From time to time the production manager would himself ask the buyer to increase these quantities, to order direct or to negotiate contracts for bulk supplies on a phased delivery basis. The net result of this lack of coordination was a great deal of friction, and a very high stores investment.

A man frequently met is the one who takes decisions and does so with alacrity, without any reference to other people. He fails to appreciate the need for coordination necessary for the organization to achieve its aims. This man receives telephone calls by mistake which do not concern him, but nevertheless probably makes a decision in an area which is not his responsibility simply because he feels capable of doing so. Not only does he do this, but he does not even tell the appropriate person that he has done it.

A gentleman of this type was encountered in a large engineering company. He was the chief designer and he would visit customers to discuss product designs. This was the prime service the company offered to their customers, and whenever the chief designer established an amendment to a design or created a new design, he would return to the company and immediately implement these changes, in many cases directly with the production foreman concerned. The net result was that a variety of designs was often produced depending on the stage of production when the chief designer made his amendments. He had no procedure for informing people about the intended changes, nor for acquainting the salesman with the new designs. Drawings were rarely updated as quickly as they should have been, and often a request for a drawing by the production department was met with what amounted to an obsolete drawing, since it did not incorporate the chief designer's amendments. Needless to say profits were affected as well as business, and not until an effective procedure was introduced for coordinating the various activities of the chief designer, the drawing office and the production departments was this problem overcome.

Recording

The office has often been criticized for its failure as a centre for maintaining records. This is one area which can be very rewarding to the observant office manager. It is very rare to find efficient filing systems and effective records. It is usual for managers to develop a form of filing which over a number of years they come to understand and use relatively efficiently. As soon as they arrive in a new office they change the filing system so that it is in line with the ones they have used previously. This is done without thought for other people who might use the system or for whether the records are being held in a logical manner for retrieval. The problem of retrieval is frequently ignored when records are filed. Customer files are often kept in numerical order, as in many large companies most of the output of computers is done on the basis of customer account number. However, when it is necessary to refer to the file, a separate operation of relating the name to the number must be carried out. How much easier to file alphabetically. But if the system cannot be changed to an alphabetical sequence, a method of cross-reference should be developed. Careful consideration should also be given to why the information is recorded, why it should be filed, how often it is referred to, in what order it is usually referred to, whether it is by customer's name, account number or numerical or alphabetical. These factors are often ignored, what is considered, however, is ease of filing. Filing is thought to be a job for a junior, an unimportant job and one which is not carried out with any degree of supervision. But let the directors be unable to locate a particular file quickly when they require it and all hell is let loose. Why blame the junior who is simply told to put things away, and is not often given adequate training?

Most offices contain large desks and beautifully designed cabinets which are totally inadequate for the filing needs of that particular function. However, the lack of effective filing equipment in offices cannot be blamed entirely on office equipment manufacturers. At the present time the range of equipment available is very extensive, and because of this perhaps it is difficult to make a reasonable choice. Some of the more sophisticated equipment is extremely expensive and, although it achieves its purpose, unless the information is filed correctly within the system, retrieval is still difficult. It is amazing how often people fail to sort correctly either numerically or alphabetically, the latter being more difficult.

Examples of misfiling are all too common for there to be a need to include any here. Other records, such as bound ledgers, books, punch cards, magnetic tapes, form part of the overall recording system, but these are normally the records held in specialist departments, the accounts department, computer department, etc., and are not readily available for general information purposes unless those in the know have been able to obtain the information from the records; in the case of punch cards, tape, etc., this requires the use of specialized equipment to convert the information into human language.

Processing

Processing of information requires relevant data, and a variety of records and processing equipment. The majority of information processing is carried out in the office, although certain aspects of direct concern to production and sales are processed by the individuals concerned. In order to process data effectively it is absolutely essential that the required output is clearly specified. This is rarely done, with the result that it is frequently necessary to have to make do with the information produced whether or not it is exactly what is required. The convenience of certain methods of data processing is determined by the processing facilities rather than the needs of the business. One meets this frequently when talking to equipment salesmen who tell you that their equipment will do this and that, but rarely ask you what is required, and rarely say their equipment can be built or altered to meet your needs.

Too much data coming into the processing function has to be rewritten or converted into a form that can be used, and too much information which comes out of the function has to be interpreted and reanalysed to be used by management. These are the difficulties which have to be overcome when designing effective data processing procedures. The aim in data processing is the production of the most useful information with the minimum of effort and as little input as possible. However, this militates against the extension of office facilities and the use of high-powered and sophisticated machinery which office managers may like to have. In order to make processing procedures speedier and more effective, additional work is created in outlying departments.

This problem occurred in a small textile firm. The accounts department was required to analyse sales by products as well as to transfer the information to the customers' accounts. The invoices which were raised by the sales office showed a multiplicity of products on each document. This, of course, required the accounts department to carry out a lengthy and laborious analysis. In order to avoid this rather lengthy analysis the accounts department requested that the sales office should issue an invoice in product groups rather than a total invoice with all products shown together.

This seemed to be a reasonable request and the sales office proceeded to produce the revised invoice format. Needless to say, the sales office had to issue three times as many invoices. The additional work created required an additional member of staff and caused additional problems in the accounts depart-ment where they now had three times as many invoices to post to the accounts, and to chase for credit control purposes. However, the analysis was certainly made much easier because the appropriate invoices could be sorted out into product groups and totalled to provide the analysis.

The interesting part of this particular problem was the fact that a copy invoice went to each representative who, in turn, analysed the sales for commission purposes and made a com-mission claim. When it was broached to the accounts depart-ment that an analysis was already being made by the sales representatives, they countered with the point that if they did not prepare an analysis 'Who was to check the salesmen's commission claim?'

Needless to say the problem was resolved with very little effort, but more of this later.

The office, as a place of work, has in recent times come under close scrutiny. It has been recognized that to work effectively people need to have the right tools and the right environment. In many instances where clerical work is required, neither the tools nor the environment are suitable and people have to make do with a situation which hardly helps efficiency. Slowly but surely companies are beginning to design and furnish offices as if they really intended that work should be done in them. Slowly but surely they are beginning to develop efficient office facilities. This question of office conditions will be considered later as it is a fundamental factor in effective paperwork control.

Moreover, to support the functions of communication, coordination, recording and processing, it is essential to provide carefully designed, well-equipped offices, and, last but not least, well-trained clerical staff.

2 The paperworker

The paperworker is a sub-species of *homo sapiens* who has evolved over the last hundred years. The paperworker lives in an office and thrives on a diet of paper. The paperworker lives a fairly monotonous life, works for very short hours and spends most of the time increasing the amount of paper which he consumes. An expedition through the office jungle will meet little opposition from him, because the paperworker is, in general terms, a docile and unimaginative creature who simply exists to process the paper flowing through the office. The aim in life of a paperworker is rather difficult to discern. It is never possible to be sure whether he tries to spend time in endless discussion on a variety of topics or whether his aim is to carry out some rather menial and ill-defined task concerned with paper.

The need for the paperworker has developed in relationship to the complexity and technical progress of industry and commerce and is principally a reflection of the attempts to meet the insatiable desire of management for information. This in itself is not necessarily a bad thing, but unless these desires are carefully specified, and unless a means of meeting them is carefully thought out and designed, the role of the paperworker will become increasingly confusing and expanded to a degree where little if anything can be achieved.

In considering the control of paperwork, the primary concern must be with the activities of the paperworker and how these can be directed with the greatest benefit to the company. In order to study these activities, the different types of paperworker which are likely to be met must be examined. There are eight main types: the creator, reader, checker, converter, filer, destroyer, fountain of knowledge, and carrier. In each of these categories an amazing degree of consistency is to be found. The following descriptions can be applied generally throughout the whole of the sub-species of paperworker, and it is hoped that from these descriptions it will be possible to identify them and understand their motivation.

The creator

It is the creator's job to produce paperwork. The amount of the creator's output and the reasons why he creates paper differ. One or two examples will be given to indicate the reasons for this particular phenomenon.

The creator may well suffer from a power complex or be a frustrated artist. Whether these are personality traits which lead to him becoming a paper creator it is difficult to decide, but there is no doubt that whatever the cause, the effect can be catastrophic.

In any organization there is enough paperwork to be processed without the efforts of the paper creator. In the majority of cases his additional effort is in areas which do little if anything to help and often reduce the profitability. If he can be controlled tremendous savings can be obtained and procedures can work far more efficiently. The paper creator tends to feel the need to show he has spent a full day in the office on the basis of the amount of paper he has created. It is not unusual to hear him boasting to his colleagues that he has sent out 150 memos and letters that day, whereas his aim should be to write nothing at all, if possible.

Individual paper creators create paper in a variety of ways. Some specialize in memos, others in copying all documents into record books and registers. Others dabble in both these methods. The overall result is the same: an increase in paperwork.

Here is an example of the memo man. The memo man feels that everything he does or says or hears must be committed to paper. As most of his time is spent listening and discussing internal matters, his great forte is the internal memo. These memos are the mainstay of this type of paper creator, especially as he frequently demands an answer which has to be in writing. Thus, the memo man causes other people to be involuntary paper creators. This man is an absolute menace, internal memos—his principal output—are a curse: internal memos should be avoided wherever possible. Those who write them in any quantity should be rigorously discouraged.

The memo man's main concern in committing everything to paper is his fear that he may have been misunderstood or misheard. He may feel that unless he writes to colleagues, they will not give him the opportunity of talking to them. He may feel that the only way he can contribute is by putting down what he thinks on paper. In many cases it has been discovered that the particular problem of the memo man is that he is often inarticulate and, therefore, uses his memo to cover up this weakness. It is, of course, necessary from time to time to send internal memos and for them to be answered. How this is done will vary, but the memo man will ensure he receives an answer by sending a further memo, even if the correspondence is addressed to colleagues in adjoining offices.

The second example of the paper creator is the book worm. The book worm believes that unless every piece of relevant information is copied into his own personal book from the document he receives, he will not be able to refer to it again or he will not be able to make use of it in carrying out his job.

The real reason the book worm enters all this information into a series of books is that he has a great fear of paper. This fear causes the book worm to enter all information he considers relevant into a form which he thinks is far more secure. A book has pages which cannot easily be lost. A book can contain only the information copied into it and not all the information written on the form. The problem with the book worm is that frequently the forms cannot be destroyed. They must be filed. They must be filed in such a way that they can be referred to. When faced with this problem the book worm will explain that if he had not got his book he would not be able to look up the form and refer to it. In most cases, of course, he never writes sufficient information in the book and it is therefore pretty useless. In addition, a book that forms a basic part of the procedures is extremely difficult to use. It means that at any one time, only one person can use the book or refer to it, and I believe it is for this reason that the book worm creates his so precious document.

The third example of the paper creator is the copier. The copier appears to have a need to make use of the latest copying machine. His call for copies of just about everything he receives or sends seems to be dictated by his obsession with the machine. The copier is identified by the fact that his files never contain originals, only photocopies. It may be that he destroys the originals or perhaps he has a file marked 'originals only to be used for copying purposes'. His whole output consists of copies. In addition to this, he sends copies to many people. His belief is that the photocopier should be fully utilized. Whether the people to whom he sends copies are concerned or whether the information on the documents is at all relevant to them seems to be totally ignored, he thus creates one of the greatest problems in paperwork. He involves people who should not be involved. Nothing takes more of a person's time than receiving a photocopy of some piece of information which is not relevant to his job, but which interests him and about which he is determined to find out more.

The memo man, the book worm and the copier are just three types of paper creator, but there are others and the following four characteristics will help to identify them all.

First, a large volume of paper memos, books, forms, copies, etc., emanating from a single paperworker indicate that he is a paper creator. Second, this man will rarely be met in a face to face situation. He rarely has time to come from his office where he is to be found copiously creating paper. Third, whenever he is met in a face to face situation at a meeting or discussion he has very little to say and is often considered to be somewhat inarticulate. Finally, if the paperwork you receive is analysed according to the sender there will be no doubt who is or is not a paper creator.

The reader

The majority of people can read, but most people read for a particular reason, perhaps to gather information for their work, to obtain enjoyment from novels, to gather knowledge from textbooks, journals or articles. However, to a few, reading is an obsession. It is an activity which they carry out to the exclusion of most others. The reader in the office causes two problems. First, he causes delay by his need to read every word in a particular document or to read a magazine from cover to cover. Not only is this delay caused by the speed of reading or by the amount of paperwork which normally passes across his desk, but by the cumulative effects of correspondence in pursuit of an answer and in the reader's desire to make use of some of the information in discussion or in writing of memos.

Incidentally, the memo man, and the reader are frequently contained in one person. How can they cram all this into one short day? The reader enjoys a good flow of correspondence and literature into his office. To ensure this he will be an avid letter writer and usually subscribes to a variety of magazines, both of which cost time and money.

The second problem with the reader is his desire to correct everything he reads. He will frequently reread a report or document in his eagerness to find yet another error. Finding and amending errors is all well and good, but when it comes to internal documentation and reports, this can provide a great area of frustration for other managers and paperworkers, especially when the correction of errors is not followed by action related to the content.

Fortunately, the reader is fairly easily identified. He is the man who always starts his discussion with, 'Have you read?' and then quotes extracts from the latest book or article. He can also be identified by the large pile of magazines and books gracing his office. A further pointer will be the constant delay in receiving replies from him or obtaining action on documentation. It is unfortunate that this individual does not find employment with a publisher reading manuscripts, there he *might* be of use, but within the majority of industrial and commercial concerns he only causes friction and annoyance and considerably reduces efficiency.

> The managing director of a firm in the Midlands was a reader. Copies of all correspondence and of a variety of documents, including payroll sheets, were sent to his department and were then sorted and filed for his attention. Although there was not very much time available, he would sit and read through this mountain of information. Most of it was, of course, purely routine.
>
> Apart from the managing director's time being employed in doing virtually a useless task it had another very disquieting effect. The managers were aware that everything they wrote or every decision they made, however routine, was brought to the managing director's attention via the correspondence and documentation procedure. They therefore made many decisions verbally which were not recorded, thus avoiding the managing director's attention. This meant that many of the firm's more important business dealings were not being properly documented and recorded. In addition to this, the managing director would spend most of his time discussing many routine unimportant matters which had come to his attention via the paperwork he received, instead of discussing the more important aspects of the business, of which he was ignorant because these were not recorded and were dealt with verbally.

The foregoing example indicates the danger of having a reader at high level. At lower levels, it is very frustrating, irritating and time wasting, but at the higher level it can be catastrophic.

The checker

The checker is a rather special kind of paperworker because procedures he develops become hidden in the overall system, and without very careful and logical analysis the problems associated with the checker cannot be easily identified. The checker creates a situation of expanded work and increased staff. Often, where people are dubbed 'empire builders', careful analysis will indicate that they are really checkers. The greatest problem caused by the checker is that, because his procedures are hidden, it is difficult to dissociate the checking activity from the data processing one.

The checker believes that every piece of information contained in a document is wrong and that nobody can do a job correctly. He believes, therefore, that it must be rigorously checked. The cost of doing this is completely ignored. The benefit of finding an error is considered to outweigh the cost factor. In most businesses, checking consumes a considerable amount of office time and its value may be open to serious question. There is no doubt that there are some areas where errors are found to occur frequently and where it is known that the benefits from checking outweigh the cost of the staff and the time involved. When such areas are found try to stop the errors occurring before accepting the need for checking.

Experience shows that when paperwork procedures are analysed, the need for checking is considerably less than anybody concerned expects. In fact, many procedures can be designed without the need for this laborious, monotonous time-consuming work. The checker, however, cannot see this. He cannot make a decision on information that has not been checked at least once and often twice or three times. In order to check it is necessary to have something against which to do so. Systems have to be developed which require filing of copies and preparing of summaries purely to check other information, all of which creates more paperwork.

Modern statistical techniques of sampling enable checking to be carried out in such a manner as to give a high degree of accuracy with a fairly low level of cost and time. Modern auditors are increasingly applying these techniques to their audit requirements. If it is of use to an auditor whose responsibility for the accuracy of information is considerable, then why is it not more readily used in normal office checking procedures?

Examples of unnecessary checking are so numerous in every business as to hardly require detailed description, but two examples from the accounts office will help to illustrate cases of generally accepted procedures which are wholly unnecessary.

I have rarely visited a company that did not check its statements. The first point in respect of this particular activity is that not all suppliers submit statements of their accounts and therefore it is not possible to completely check all accounts. The checking of a statement from a supplier against the information that has been extracted from invoices and posted to the ledger usually takes place two or three months after the actual transaction. If a difference occurs, this would normally indicate that an invoice had not been recorded and thus the supplier had not received the full amount of his account.

Now it is normal for all suppliers to query an overdue amount. This query is frequently received at about the time the statements are checked or in some cases before they have been checked, while action in adjusting accounts or asking for copy invoices is almost entirely taken from letters requesting payment rather than from errors found on statements. If the systems are correct, then payments to the supplier will normally be correct and any differences will be pointed out by the supplier in his letters asking for payment. There are reasons given why statement checking is useful, but all these can be discounted on the basis that it serves nothing and just consumes additional clerical time. It is doubtful if there has ever been an instance where statement checking was of any benefit whatsoever.

Another checking job found in the accounts office is the checking of extensions on suppliers' invoices. This, of course, assumes that suppliers cannot work out the value of their invoices correctly. From time to time errors are made and these may be either of benefit to the supplier or of benefit to the company concerned and perhaps swings and roundabouts would eliminate them. Certainly, in any instance where one meets extension checking and asks the question, 'How many errors have been found?' the answer is usually none or very few. In those instances where errors are found, it almost always concerns a few suppliers who do not have the facilities for proper extension of invoices. If the suspect suppliers can be established, then it is possible to limit the checking to those invoices which experience indicates are likely to be wrong. But does this happen? No! All invoices, all extensions are checked; statistical techniques of sampling are not applied. These sampling techniques simply require the selection of a number of invoices from a supplier, checking over a period of time and estimating what degree of accuracy is being achieved.

Apart from the money-saving aspect of using sampling techniques there is the personnel aspect. Normally comptometer operators or clerks with calculators are involved in checking extensions and in totalling, and it is soul-destroying to do a job the sole purpose of which is to find errors which do not often occur. The result is that they are quite pleased to find a mistake, almost regardless of whether it is beneficial or otherwise, and disappointed to find everything correct. After a while it begins to dawn on them that perhaps this is not a wholly necessary job, and nothing can be more frustrating than to find one is spending time on unnecessary work.

The checker can be identified by the numerous rubber stamps saying 'checked by', 'passed to', etc., which can be found on his desk and the provision of facilities on the forms with which he is concerned for initials when the information has been checked. He usually controls a fairly large staff of junior checkers and is normally associated with the accounts office. He may have a background of auditing from years past or he may on some occasion have worked in a bank, where extensive checking is essential. This type of background is often the cause of his present problem.

The converter

Converters come in many forms, with many different titles and descriptions, but all can be recognized by their one action of conversion of data from one form to another. They add nothing to the data which they handle; they do not process data, they do not improve data and in many cases they make it less readable. The function of the converter adds nothing to efficient office methods. In general, the converter is not to blame. It is the fault of the management for requiring conversion of data in the first place. There are occasions, for instance, when it is considered necessary to have written communication and it is important that what is written is readable. But where the communication is handwritten and is readable, it is pointless to convert from longhand into typescript.

Complaints are made today that the machine is taking over from the human being. If this complaint is valid, then it is because people are losing the ability to do themselves what they can rely on a machine to do. Indeed, typewritten material can be read more easily than handwriting, so why not write straight on to a small typewriter rather than use a pen, the need for a copy typist or some other form of converter is then avoided. The invention of shorthand has been a boon. No longer does the creator of the material have to write it down for it to be copied. He dictates to a girl who takes it down in her own way as quickly as the writer can speak, and she then converts it from that almost indecipherable scribble into typewritten form.

However, shorthand itself creates problems. The shorthand typist has become a new breed of converter. Because she converts the spoken word into a form only decipherable by a highly trained person she has become available only at a premium. This has led to the increasing use of dictating machines and audio typists, with shorthand typists being reserved for those managers who cannot get used to using dictating machines, often because they do not speak fluently enough to be decipherable from a tape. Or is it because shorthand typists are generally more attractive than dictating machines?

Audio typing is perhaps the most efficient means of converting the spoken word to the written word and if operated correctly is very efficient. However, industry and commerce are still employing shorthand and copy typists, as well as audio typists. Although the demand may be increasing for the last there seems to be no lack of demand few, if any, of which are concerned with improving office efficiency.

The following examples indicate two types of unnecessary conversion which are all too prevalent in offices, but which still go unrecognized.

The correction of customers' accounts was carried out in one business by the initial correction being handled by the sales office concerned who completed a correction advice in duplicate and sent the top copy to the head office sales department. In this department the correction advice was copied by a clerk who entered details on to a draft credit note. This was required by the typists. The draft credit note was sent to the typists with the correction advice attached. It was then typed on to a three-part credit note which was returned to the sales department who checked the typed credit note with the draft credit note. When this had been corrected and was ready to be sent out, the procedure was to send the top copy to the customer, the second copy to the district sales office and to file the third copy with the correction advice. At the end of the week, a list of credit notes and their value was made. This was sent to the computer department where the information was punched ready to go into the sales accounts.

A good deal of the conversion work was eliminated when the credit notes were prepared at the district sales office, a copy sent to the customer, a copy filed and a copy sent to the computer department to be punched for the sales accounts.

A second example is that of an executive in a large company who did not like to receive or to send handwritten communications. This particular dislike was so great that incoming handwritten reports and memos were retyped by his secretary before he would look at them. On occasions she retyped memos which when read by the executive were destroyed or filed with no particular use being made of the information. If one were to consider the proportion of incoming to outgoing correspondence the secretary spent most of her time typing incoming handwritten communications. When other executives who sent handwritten communications heard of this they decided that there was little point in making the effort to save on conversion costs by writing their reports in longhand. They began to have them typed. This meant that they required the services of a typist or secretary and the situation was exacerbated. No solution was found to this problem as the executive concerned was in a position to ensure a continuation of the practice.

One converter who has not been mentioned in these two examples is the clerk, who is often involved in the transposition of data from one form to another doing little to it in the process. This has got to be recognized as conversion rather than processing and requires a good deal of careful analysis to identify the difference. Punch operators are required only to convert written human information into machine-readable data.

At present there are only a few types of input available which do not require this form of conversion. In time it is likely that more sophisticated machines will be developed to allow direct human input to the machine. At present one of the main forms of direct input is mark sensing, which requires training to use and specially prepared documents. Another form is a direct input terminal which requires less training, but is part of an expensive configuration. These terminals take the form of typewriter consoles or visual display screens through which information can be transferred to the computer. However, it is not proposed to list all the mechanical aids for the furtherance of paperwork, but to indicate how to control the problems of paperwork itself. Whether modern machines overcome these problems or simply hide them behind the apparent efficiency of the equipment is another matter. A great deal of work in offices is simply converting data from one form to another. I consider some 25 per cent of time spent on paperwork is concerned with converting data.

The filer

There are two categories of filer. The first type of filer is the person who decides that the files are necessary. The second type is the one whose responsibility it is to put the appropriate documents into the file, with the hope of extracting the data when required. At home the file creator always has a crammed attic. He cannot throw anything away, which is the main problem associated with filing in most companies. He is not generally concerned with the form his filing system takes. In extreme cases, he develops a sophisticated system which only he can understand. The file creator believes that a copy of every document or every communication passing across his desk must be filed as a permanent record. This requires a good deal of equipment, and it requires a means of informing the file filler what to do with the document, in particular where to file it.

Many people do not even do this. They rely entirely on the file filler to place the document in the appropriate file. In many cases, a person carrying out this job is not usually in a position to make a decision as to which is the correct file. The result of this is that there is an accumulation of a great deal of useless paper. This fills drawers, cupboards, cabinets which occupy considerable office space. Having produced a space problem, it may then be decided to use a more sophisticated type of equipment and to microfilm all the files thus reducing the space problem. The fact that the problem could simply have been solved by compressing the files in a baling machine or by throwing them away never seems to be considered.

The work of the file creator can be seen in any office. No examples are necessary. It will suffice to say that it takes up approximately 20 per cent of all clerical activity. The file filler may be in the invidious position of filing documents which may be required by management. It is the performance of this job which causes problems when we come to retrieve the documents concerned. People are rarely trained to file correctly, it is normally done by a junior. This of course creates its own problems.

The filing of temporary storage data which are used within the department is normally done by the people within the department who need the information to be readily available, and is usually reasonably efficient, but once again it often employs junior staff and thus retrieval is often hindered by lack of filing ability.

The simple tests I have carried out have shown that people cannot sort easily into alphabetical order which is vital for accurate filing, nor can they speedily sort in numerical order, although this is by far the most accurate sequence for filing. Often an absurd situation results where people try to file numerically and alphabetically by issuing blocks of numbers. This is doomed to total failure, unless one leaves so much space in the numerical blocks as to make the numerical sequence absolutely useless.

The retrieval of information held in file absorbs a further 15 per cent of clerical activity. It can be seen therefore that up to now in the examination of paperwork a total of 60 per cent of clerical time has been absorbed in the activities of checking, filing and retrieval of information. This only leaves 40 per cent of clerical activity for the more important activities of data processing and communication.

The destroyer

The destroyer is the counterpart of the filer, only he carries this to such an extent that he is the cause of a great deal of strife. He destroys paperwork to the point where necessary documentation is eliminated. He cries for efficiency and in so doing removes from the offices much important documentation. His aims are to be admired, in that he is striving to eliminate a good deal of paperwork. His methods, however, require careful examination. Not to reply to communications which require it causes additional demands for an answer. The destroyer frequently uses the excuse that he has not received a document. He may well forget destroying it because he acts without thinking when he throws paper into his waste-paper basket. It is these factors surrounding the destroyer's activities which cause the trouble. He never seems to have a copy of a report. It is always necessary to obtain a further copy when these reports are being considered in meetings or discussions. He may claim to have been omitted from the circulation list, even though he has destroyed that particular document. In most offices his activities can be overcome with the help of the secretary or staff servicing his requirements. In this case, unknown to the destroyer, they can maintain files of communications and correspondence which they know or believe to be necessary and should be kept on file. With a little experience of the destroyer, it is fairly reasonable to develop this secondary filing system in order to cover his activity.

One of the worst faults of the destroyer is that he never informs other people concerned in the system that he is eliminating a document. He probably does not consider that the person to whom the document is to go has a need for the information it contains. This is a very major cause of criticism that can be levelled at the so-called 'office efficiency man'. He makes the decision without consultation, but he is not experienced enough or able to make careful logical analysis of the systems or paper requirements, and takes an *ad hoc* view of what should be destroyed.

When faulty systems are met, or when departments are failing to carry out procedures, it is necessary to look first of all for a destroyer. It may be his activities which are causing some of the basic problems.

On page 23 the system for handling credit notes was outlined. Having made the amendments indicated in that example, part of the system was not functioning correctly, and this was eventually attributed to the fact that one of the local sales offices boasted a destroyer who did not consider that it was necessary to send copies to head office. He never bothered to find out what use was made of the copy at head office and, consequently, notification of credits were not received by the computer department. Information was not punched and posted to the customer's account and the credit control department were still chasing money for which credit notes had already been issued. This caused annoyance to the customer and also a great deal of correspondence between the head office, the sales office and the customer.

The fountain of knowledge

There is usually one fountain of knowledge in every office. He takes it upon himself to obtain information on all the company's activities. He does this by demanding to be on all circulation lists in order to receive information from many sources about the company's activities. He insists on verbal as well as written information. The purpose of collecting all this data appears to be his desire to be able to tell other people in the company what is happening. He achieves major success when he can inform someone of a change in their working situation of which they are as yet unaware. He is constantly heard to complain that he was not told about something. He never considers the relevance of the information to his basic job. He combines the roles and the problems of the reader and the filer; the work he creates is considerable. He normally has to have staff to deal with his correspondence and filing. He is rarely off the telephone and can, in many cases, be said to be the root of the grapevine. 'If you want to know anything, ask Joe.'

This man may appear to have his uses, and unless we examine how he collects all his information and achieves his position as the fountain of knowledge it is possible to be deceived into thinking that he plays a useful role. If communications were operating successfully there would be no need for the fountain of knowledge. In most companies the attitude taken towards matters which are very confidential and matters of interest to the staff are never correctly balanced. When change is about to take place in the office, this individual can cause great problems. Perhaps a department is being reorganized for the sake of greater efficiency and that this is being done quietly, carefully and slowly without unsettling the staff. But the fountain of knowledge, in his endeavour to be successful, discloses the information and may well cause people to become worried about the likely effect of the change.

Examples of this person's activities are often met, and there is no doubt he is one of the major obstacles in reorganizing offices. His activities, if allowed to continue unchecked, can reach the stage where his imagination may run riot. Through his desire to constantly furnish new information, he will fabricate information, which causes the disruption of normal office procedures. The work he must do in order to gather information also has a disrupting effect and causes a great deal of unnecessary communication within the office. Thus, the apparent usefulness of the fountain of knowledge must be disregarded as he is likely more often than not to produce poisoned water.

The carrier

The flow of paperwork can reach such a level that people have to be employed solely to carry paper from one destination to another.

Many large offices have introduced pneumatic paper conveying systems which ensure that paper can be carried more quickly than ever. It is said to save a great deal of time and there is no doubt that using people to convey paper is a slow process. Frequently, they deliver their loads amid a great deal of discussion and conversation. They play a key part in the grapevine, and it is amazing how long it takes for a message sent by telex, which may have travelled thousands of miles in a matter of seconds, to reach its final destination by hand. The whole point of sophisticated communications equipment is to transfer information quickly. These delays are not, of course, the fault of the paper carrier. It is really the fault of the practice of conveying paper in this way. It can be almost completely avoided by asking the appropriate personnel to collect their mail and other communications from a central point. This is much more efficient than it may sound. It is possible at the same time to deposit communications for other people in the appropriate pigeon hole. Naturally, senior executives would expect their secretaries to collect their correspondence.

It is always necessary to transfer systems documentation from one department to another and, in an open office, from one section to another. This is usually best done as the final operation of handling. When the work is completed it is taken to the section for which it is intended, instead of waiting for someone else to remove it. In an open office, examples can be seen of piles of documents remaining on a desk awaiting the post girl, while, at the other side of the room, a girl is sitting waiting to work on the same documents. It appears that getting up and walking with documents and delivering them to the appropriate point is deemed to be a very lowly task. But look around the office and see how many senior executives walk from office to office carrying papers of some description or another. In chapter 8 I will describe how properly designed offices and systems can almost completely eliminate the necessity for the paper carrier.

This chapter has discussed the paperworker at some length. It has described several different types of paperworkers, indicating how they add to the flow of paper in the organization, and how, if they would only consider the effect of their action, paperwork could be considerably reduced. Part 3 of this book will consider the control of the paperworker, indicating how proper methods can be employed which eliminate most of the problems outlined in this chapter. In all the examples which have been given of different types of paper-worker, part of their time has certainly been spent doing the job for which they are being paid. It is the fact that these jobs are done which enables most offices to function. The end result of the activities of these paperworkers is the employment of considerably more staff than necessary. This is why, with the growth and complexity of industry and commerce, it is becoming increasingly important to examine all staff additions.

Information is becoming a vital resource of industry and commerce. What is meant is *relevant, accurate* information, and this can only be obtained by using carefully designed systems. If the paperworkers are allowed to continue their activities unchecked, they are going to develop almost unworkable and, at best, inefficient systems which may never produce accurate or relevant information. It is of major importance to understand the reasons for the activities of paper-workers and to then develop a cure if required. Many pointers will be given later as to how this can be done. It is hoped that this area will be very carefully examined. All businesses show some of the symptoms of paperworker activity. But it is an activity that can be controlled; it is really only the extreme cases which will have to be dealt with by surgery.

Part 2
Controlling paperwork

3 In the beginning

Effective control of paperwork cannot be achieved by panic measures instituted when things become too chaotic for the normal routine processing of data. To control paperwork, it is necessary to have an attitude of mind towards all aspects of administration together with a basis of well-designed, practical and simple procedures. When most companies start life they have very little need for paper. Only the most essential documentation is tolerated. Customers' orders are taken verbally as well as in writing, and the minimum of necessary work for invoicing and collecting of money is carried out. The primary concern of the owners is the extension of their business, and this does not allow time for the accumulation of too many pieces of paper. As the company develops, it becomes more and more impracticable for the owners to control every transaction. When they delegate or transfer responsibility for carrying out certain activities to subordinates, they start the paper trail. From this point on it is necessary for paper to be used, primarily to ensure effective communication and coordination of activities, and, more importantly, to make up for the lack of trust which is the primary cause for the majority of paper.

After a while, any successful company rapidly reaches a stage where many people are employed in handling paper, paper, which in earlier years, would have been totally unnecessary. Is it the people who create the paper, or the paper which creates the need for people? This is a question which will gradually be resolved as this book proceeds.

In the beginning, there is no doubt that the company gave more attention to making decisions and handling information in order to carry out the basic operations and to satisfy the customers' orders, little attention was given to paper. So why were various documents and procedures ever introduced? What was their purpose? What was their value? There would have been, of course, some areas where the lack of paper caused problems. Can those areas now be identified? It is necessary for the present procedures to be taken apart, to establish the activities which are desirable and necessary for the company to function properly. This can often mean going back to look at how things were done, why there were changes and the benefits that these changes achieved.

It is necessary to study the development of the company to obtain an understanding of how the systems have been evolved. Were the developments made in order to cure real problems or imaginary ones? Many questions must be asked in order to understand how existing procedures have developed. You may think that knowing how systems have developed is not relevant to the question of whether they are efficient now. But can improvements be made without knowing how that system has developed? The answer is 'No'. It is difficult if not impossible to take a procedure and redesign it successfully without understanding its aims.

It is essential, therefore, that if the right place to begin to control paperwork is to be found, the origin of the systems are examined. This history will not always be available. With takeovers and amalgamations of companies, the details of their procedure developments may be lost. In addition, the reasons for the development of systems are never adequately recorded. If the people who started them have left, this kind of information is lost. In this case, the only answer one receives when asking why something is done in a particular way is that it has always been done that way so far as anyone knows.

In order to start the control of paperwork and of administrative procedures, it is essential to carry out two detailed enquiries. The first is to find out what paper is used by the company. The second is to find out what people do. It is amazing how many employers are unaware what their employees do. This can be answered by saying that the boss should not be concerned with details which can safely be left to a subordinate. However, a good subordinate can be very difficult to find. When he is found, he may often be one of the paperworkers mentioned previously and hardly engenders any confidence as far as procedures are concerned.

What paper is used?

This enquiry involves collecting a sample of every piece of paper which is handled by the company. This means all internal and external forms and several categories of correspondence. The collection is itself a rather tedious task, and should be carried out with the aid of a photocopier where necessary so as to avoid taking documents in current use out of the system. The value of documents must be established which should be tackled in three stages.

The first step is to indicate the purpose of each form on the reverse side. When a particular document cannot be categorized in this way a large question mark must be put on it. This should be done without consulting the actual users of the document. It is done by the manager or the person assigned to the enquiry, who should have sufficient knowledge of the business to assess the use of the various forms.

Step two is to sort the forms into three sections; those which are necessary, those which are unnecessary and those which carry a question mark. In each list of forms is marked the department handling that form (see Fig. 3.1).

The third step is one in which the source and preparation of the forms are analysed. This is done by using a separate sheet designed to collect the relevant information (see Fig. 3.2). The form detail sheet is the basic record for further analysis both in this enquiry and the later more detailed assignments.

When this enquiry has been completed, a considerable amount of data will have been collected which is used in deciding where to start

SHEET NO.

FORM TITLE	PURPOSE	SOURCE	RECORDED IN	FILED IN	USED BY

Fig. 3.1   Form analysis

FORM TITLE		SOURCE	
PURPOSE			
COPIES	DISTRIBUTION		PURPOSE

DEPARTMENT	DATA ENTERED	DATA EXTRACTED

DATA CARRIED

TIMING

PLACE WHERE FORM FILED	REFERRED TO BY:	PERIOD FORM RETAINED	VOLUME PER MONTH

Fig. 3.2   Form detail sheet

controlling paperwork. The data available indicates the documents used, where they come from, what they are used for and the quantities required. In addition, there is a series of forms for which a use cannot be found and a series for which the use is questionable. These two aspects will lead fairly quickly to the areas most in need of detailed examination. In deciding where to begin a more detailed examination, the following factors should be isolated:

36

1. Lack of purpose
2. Duplication of purpose
3. Duplication of data
4. Duplication of records and files
5. High volumes
6. Importance of the documents
7. Wide distribution of forms

A survey of forms used was carried out in a large chemical company. It took several days to collect all the forms. These were on first examination categorized as follows:

Necessary: 74
Doubtful use: 100
No apparent use: 106

Further examination to prepare the form detail sheet indicated that many forms were still being prepared by departments who had not been informed that they were obsolete. In addition, several doubtful forms were, on re-examination, found to be necessary, and several forms with no apparent use became doubtful. The picture was now:

Necessary: 86
Doubtful use: 110
No apparent use: 30

When duplication of purpose and content were examined, the following final summary of forms was prepared for detailed critical analysis:

Necessary:	86	including 26 apparent duplications
Doubtful:	110	including 86 apparent duplications
No apparent use:	NIL	all had been considered unnecessary duplications of other forms

Even before starting the detailed survey, the number of forms had been reduced on paper from 280 to 196. Steps were taken immediately to effect this reduction and to examine in depth the purchasing and stores procedures which accounted for 23 of the necessary forms and 46 of the doubtful forms.

Who does what?

Who does what is an enquiry directly related to the various functions of every administrative department. The paperwork created by people not normally employed to do paperwork must also be examined. In this way a complete picture is created of where the work is done both in terms of situation and in terms of departmental sections. This cannot be done by merely sitting down with section heads, foremen or departmental managers. It is possible that they will not know clearly what their subordinates are doing. They may think they know. They may assume that instructions which they have issued in the past are being carried out, but this may not be so. All too frequently procedures are misinterpreted or systems are changed slightly as time passes, so that eventually it is very difficult to say clearly what people are doing in the kind of detail that is required for this enquiry.

The most effective approach is to obtain from the department head an indication of what each section in his department does, from the section head an account of what each clerk does, and then from each clerk find out what they actually do. It is almost certain that all three will differ in emphasis and in content.

DEPARTMENT						
INDIVIDUAL	ACTIVITY	FORMS USED	FILES USED	RECORDS USED	OTHER INFORMATION USED	SOURCE

Fig. 3.3   Activity schedule

The sequence of questions should be as follows, and to assist the interviewer a questionnaire should be prepared for each clerk.

What do you do?
What documents do you receive?
              . . . create?
              . . . file?
              . . . distribute?
What records do you keep?
What files do you keep?
How many documents do you handle?
How often do you refer to the files?
How long do you spend on each aspect of the job?

It is possible that answers to the questionnaire could be completed by each clerk concerned, but this practice should be avoided if possible to ensure accurate and coherent answers. The use of a simple record sheet (Fig. 3.3) will help in the subsequent analysis of who does what.

From the information collected it will be seen that clerical activities fall mainly into the following categories:

Communicating
Writing
Sorting
Filing
Copying
Checking
Calculating

In-depth examination of these activities throughout the organization will lead ultimately to the control of paperwork. It must be stressed that, in carrying out these two initial surveys, it is essential to find the most beneficial areas to commence detailed studies. It is possible to tackle problem areas individually as they appear, but the separate solutions will not necessarily provide a complete answer.

Treating symptoms brings about short-term relief, but careful and accurate diagnosis of the problem is the only way to find a cure.

It is apparent that a great deal of time is spent collecting information. It is appropriate to pause here to consider the principal way this is done, namely, by interviewing.

Interviewing

The skill required by the interviewer is considerable. He has to deal with many types of people in widely differing situations. His purpose is to obtain facts, verify the facts, obtain ideas and opinions and establish contact. The interviewer has to be impartial, tactful, a good listener, a good conversationalist and be skilful in soliciting answers. There is no short-cut to becoming a successful interviewer, but the following pointers should help.

CONDUCTING THE INTERVIEW

Use simple terms
Create interest and attention
Use occasional compliments
Never criticize
Do not appear superior
Be polite and well mannered
Make the interviewee feel important
Go to the interviewee's office
Above all, be honest

DEVELOPING A GOOD DESK-SIDE MANNER

Give full attention to the interviewee
Listen patiently without interruption
Never argue
Never give advice
Plan the interview
Present a summary to the interviewee for agreement and clarification
Explain that personal notes are confidential

Keep control and move towards a logical ending by recapitulating carefully and by suggesting a possible further visit to provide answers on any points which the interviewer has missed.

The good interviewer knows how to deal with the problems of interviewing. People react to being questioned in a variety of ways, and an ability to weigh up the interviewee is a valuable asset. Some of the more frequently encountered problems are considered below.

The inability of the interviewee to explain what he does can be overcome by asking him to demonstrate how he does his job. This approach can avoid a good deal of embarrassment.

If the interviewee is over-talkative, he should be kept to the point by careful questioning.

Exaggeration of volume of work and over-justification for records and activities may be an indication of an empire builder. The interviewer must use his skill and a good deal of tact and diplomacy to establish the facts.

When answers are not readily forthcoming, the interviewer has to be patient and sympathetic in order to instil confidence and overcome the fears of the interviewee.

Suggesting that the interviewee's experience is vital to the successful completion of the assignment often provides a basis for talking to the long-service employee who shows a reluctance to explain what he does.

Shyness is overcome by the interviewer adopting a friendly and reassuring attitude.

People are often uneasy about being interviewed and try to forestall the dreaded event by becoming too busy. This can be overcome by suggesting that the aim of the survey is to establish why the interviewee is overworked and how this can be resolved. In addition, the interviewer should ensure than an appropriate time is chosen for the interview, i.e., not at the clerk's busiest time of day.

Complaints and criticisms of other people and departments will be made to the interviewer by certain employees. The interviewer must be careful to appear neutral and non-committal and yet listen in a sympathetic manner because some of the problems may be real.

The interviewee's use of jargon or technical detail often covers up his difficulty in talking about his work. The interviewer must overcome this by explaining that he is unaware of the meaning of the terms and could the interviewee please explain them. This gives the latter confidence and leads to an easier conversation.

The problem of direct antagonism and objection to being interviewed is not often met, especially if the interviewer is skilled. Where it is met the interviewer must ask the employee why he does not want to talk about his job and should indicate that it is of general benefit for the discussion to take place. A useful approach is to ask the person concerned to write a synopsis of his job so that the interview can be kept short and to the point. The interviewer's sympathetic and polite approach will usually overcome the objections. Active hostility must be avoided and if none of the above tactics are successful then the information must be obtained elsewhere.

One of my most difficult interviewing experiences was encountered in the stores office of an engineering company in the

Midlands. The storekeeper was en ex-army sergeant who believed that the only way to run the stores was the way he had learnt in the army. He exercised strict discipline on the staff both in the office and in the stores. He insisted that he should attend each interview to ensure that the right answers were forthcoming. The three office staff lived in awe of their supervisor, and it was quite clear that an interview, as suggested by the storekeeper, was going to be of little purpose.

I suggested to the storekeeper that he should be interviewed with his own superior in attendance. His attitude was predictably hostile to this suggestion, but he saw the point and agreed to his staff being interviewed in private as long as he received a detailed report of each interview. This was refused and the previous argument was used together with the explanation that notes taken were confidential. As the interviews proceeded a varied picture of the work carried out in the stores office emerged. It transpired that a great deal of time was being spent on the maintenance of complete stock records for many small items and for single purchases for special jobs which were booked in and out. The final summary of the work done was agreed by the storekeeper with some pride and a certain degree of friendship. The comments, opinions, complaints and criticisms of his staff remained in the notes for further examination at a later date.

There is no sure method of becoming a good interviewer, but if the above points are kept in mind they should be a considerable help towards it. This is one area where practice is the only way to learn.

The key to successful control of paperwork is a knowledge of the paper used in the business and of the clerical activities concerned with handling that paper. The first two enquiries have provided the basic knowledge needed to determine where to start the process of detailed and critical analysis of each aspect of the procedures.

4 The pathfinder

The calf path

One day through the primeval wood
a calf walked home as good calves should;
But made a trail all bent askew,
A crooked trail as all calves do.
Since then three hundred years have fled,
And I infer the calf is dead.
But still he left behind his trail
And thereby hangs my moral tale.

But the trail was taken up next day
By a lone dog that passed that way;
And then a wise bell-wether sheep
Pursued the trail o'er vale and steep,
And drew the flock behind him too,
as good bell-wethers always do.

And from that day, o'er hill and glade,
Through those old woods a path was made,
And many men wound in and out
And dodged and turned and bent about,
And uttered words of righteous wrath
Because 'twas such a crooked path.
But still they followed—do not laugh—
The first migrations of that calf,
And through this winding roadway stalked
Because he wobbled when he walked.

This forest path became a lane
That bent and turned and turned again;
This crooked lane became a road
Where many a poor horse with his load
Toiled beneath the burning sun,
And travelled some three miles in one;

And thus a century and a half
They trod in the footsteps of that calf.

The years passed on in swiftness fleet,
The road became a village street;
And this, before men were aware,
A city's crowded thoroughfare.
And soon the central street was this
of a renowned metropolis;
And men two centuries and a half
Trod in the footsteps of that calf.

Each day a hundred thousand rout
Followed this zig-zag calf about—;
And o'er his crooked journey went
The traffic of a continent.
A hundred thousand men were led
By one calf near three centuries dead.

They followed still his crooked way,
And lost one hundred years a day;
For thus such a reverence is lent
To well established precedent.
A moral lesson this might teach,
Were I ordained and called to preach.
For men are prone to go it blind
Along the calf paths of the mind,
And work away from sun to sun,
To do what other men have done.
They follow in the beaten track
And out and in, and forth and back,
And still their devious course pursue,
To keep the path that others do.
They keep the path and sacred groove
Along which all their lives they move,
But how the wise old wood-gods laugh
Who saw the first primeval calf.
Ah! many things this tale might teach
But I am not ordained to preach.

Sam Walter Foss

To identify the calf path is the problem facing most pathfinders at
work in industry and commerce. The role of the pathfinder is not an
easy one. Systems have paths which, when drawn on paper, look like

the string puzzles often seen in children's comics. A pathfinder's problem is to discover what the paths are at present, so that he can question the necessity for the direction which is now taken. These paths may have been developed over a number of years, and have developed frequently in an *ad hoc* manner without due regard for the effect on the overall system. Thus, the system ends up with not one small path, but with a main path with many side paths, some leading to a dead end. In the face of this, inexperienced pathfinders often balk at the seeming complexity and multiplicity of forms and procedures which face them. Are they following a calf path or are they not?

It is pertinent to consider the attributes which the successful pathfinder needs before he can hope to trace the paths winding in and out of all office procedures. The following list of qualities has been collected from a variety of written material. The pathfinder must:

1. Have an analytical mind
2. Be creative
3. Be a good salesman
4. Have management potential
5. Be objective
6. Be thick-skinned
7. Be tactful
8. Be patient
9. Have the ability to apply common sense
10. Be sceptical in order to chase for facts not fiction
11. Have a sense of humour
12. Be enthusiastic and optimistic
13. Be self-reliant
14. Be tenacious
15. Be imaginative
16. Be open-minded
17. Be a good conversationalist
18. Be a clear and concise writer
19. Have an ability to display courage in the face of over-whelming odds

Whether such a superman exists is highly doubtful, I have never met one. Given that to do the job needs so many qualities, no wonder most people consider the task of the pathfinder an almost impossible one, but if one accepts this premise, the problem will never be tackled.

The pathfinder's main role is to talk to and to examine the activities of other people. When dealing with people, many of the above attributes will, of course, be extremely useful. However, sitting back waiting for a man who has them all to appear is not the answer. In the larger companies, it is possible to select one or two men who can specialize in this type of work, and because of this can each develop some of the qualities outlined above. For the smaller company, however, it may be impossible to employ somebody especially to do the pathfinder's job. If this is so, the owner or manager should study to acquire these qualities and take the steps outlined in this book to rationalize the company's paperwork.

The assignment brief

Whether or not the task is to be faced by the manager or owner, or by an employee, it must be tackled by someone with a deep interest in what he has to do. The steps indicated in this book should be followed if any improvement is to be achieved in the many varied and complex paperwork procedures which exist in industry and commerce.

The first two enquiries provide information concerning the forms used in the business, and the activities of the people concerned with paperwork, and this information is also useful in examining procedures selected for detailed study. From this, it is possible to sit down and make an overall assessment of the time the survey will take.

However, before the pathfinder starts he must prepare, with the help of the management, a written statement which clearly sets down the purpose of the procedures under examination (Fig. 4.1). It may seem odd that it is necessary to put this in writing, but only in this way does the real purpose of this system emerge and enable the pathfinder to assess whether the procedures are relevant.

In a medium-sized woodwork company, the sales procedures were to be examined in detail. In designing the brief (or the summary of purpose), the sales manager was asked what the purpose of the procedure was. 'Ah', he said, 'that is an interesting question, the purpose of the procedure is to ensure the information regarding the sale of the goods is transmitted to the accounts department, so that they can obtain payment from the customer.'

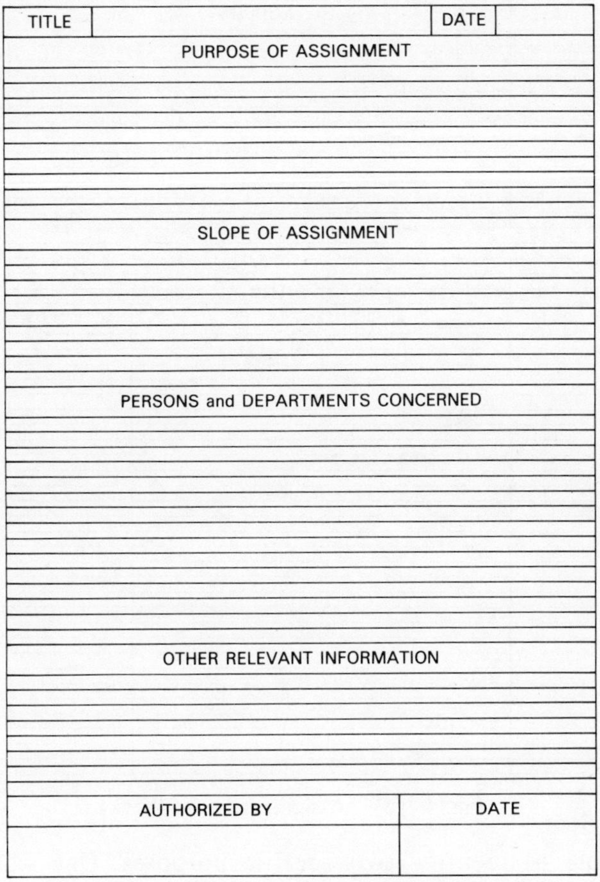

TITLE		DATE	
PURPOSE OF ASSIGNMENT			

SLOPE OF ASSIGNMENT

PERSONS and DEPARTMENTS CONCERNED

OTHER RELEVANT INFORMATION

AUTHORIZED BY	DATE

Fig. 4.1(a)   Assignment brief (front)

Then the accountant was questioned, he reiterated this and said, 'Ah yes, that is the purpose of the procedure'.

The sales manager was asked whether or not he was interested in what he had sold and to whom. 'Well, of course I am,' he said, 'that is vital information, without which I doubt very much whether any of our sales plans would be of much value.' He was asked how he obtained this information. 'It is a by-product of the sales accounting system.' He was asked which was the most vital piece of information to him. 'The details of sales, of course.' When it was suggested that the invoicing of customers was a by-product of the sales statistical system he said, 'Now that is an interesting point, I had never looked at it in that way.' Regardless of which was the right purpose it was

ASSIGNMENT TIMETABLE	
DATE	ACTIVITY

DATE	ASSIGNMENT NOTES	ACTION BY

Fig. 4.1(b)   Assignment brief (back)

possible to identify two specific purposes. One was the collection of sales information, the other was the invoicing of the customer, both important, both specific purposes which had to be achieved. Neither was a by-product of the other, both had to be built into an effective system.

Having decided the purpose, the next task is to decide the objects or scope of the assignment. There are four main possibilities:

1. It may be to reduce costs and/or
2. To increase efficiency in terms of clerical effort
3. It may be to achieve the declared purpose, not at present achieved
4. It may be to provide more effective and relevant information.

These are not necessarily easy to achieve. For instance, in order to achieve the declared purpose one may have to spend more money on staff and equipment, and in order to provide more effective information, one may also need to spend money. But, too often, companies are more interested in reducing costs rather than in spending money to create an effective system. The next section covers the people and the departments concerned. This information should already be available from the initial enquiries, but it may need supplementing in order to deal with interacting departments which do not appear to be involved initially. Other relevant information deals with documents used, and any reference to existing instruction sheets or procedure manuals should be mentioned.

Finally, the pathfinder must decide upon the approach to the assignment. How he is going to tackle it and how long will it take?

There are various opinions about the preparation of this brief and who should prepare it, but I strongly recommend that it should be prepared by the pathfinder. Of course, he will do so in discussion with the managers concerned, but if he is to carry out a worthwhile project, he must be involved in deciding what the aims are and in setting down the approach to the project.

Figures 4.1(a) and 4.1(b) indicate the front and back of an assignment brief. The bottom part of the back page contains a section for assignment notes. It is essential that the pathfinder records his activities and the meetings and discussions which take place with the dates, etc., on the reverse of the brief so that the whole of the assignment is recorded in the one document. Having done all these things, the pathfinder must obtain formal authorization in the form of the signature of the manager responsible on the bottom of the assignment brief.

Following the path: where to begin

The pathfinder is now ready to begin his tracking exercise. The first stage is to decide at which end of the path he will start. Does he start at the beginning with the creation of the document or at the end with the final destruction or permanent filing of the document concerned? Because it is more difficult to trace a system backwards than to trace it forwards, I would always suggest starting at the beginning of the life of a form or a procedure. For example, in a purchase procedure the beginning would be the request for the materials from inside the company, whereas for a sales procedure it would be the order placed by the customer. The pathfinder has now to carry out a logical and careful examination of each part of the route followed by the documentation and the data it contains.

During the exercise he is looking for a variety of clues which reveal the use to which the information is put and the amount of effort used in order to carry out the procedure. He does this by asking a series of questions. This entails a considerable amount of detailed interviewing in respect of both the documentation and of the activities being carried out. It is essential that the questions should follow a logical sequence. One question must lead to another in such a manner that the answers can be recorded in a form which allows subsequent analysis. Failure to do this provides a series of unrelated, disjointed answers which it is extremely difficult to coordinate.

This question and answer technique can lead the pathfinder not only through complex procedures to his ultimate aim of a complete picture, but will also be useful on occasions when the procedures are not complex, when they may only involve one or two documents and be straightforward.

In the interviewing and the questioning process the pathfinder receives a vast amount of information in the form of answers, opinions and attitudes. A good deal will be fictional, but a good deal will be fact. He has to take note of most of this information and to do so in a manner which allows him to filter it at a later date in order to extract the relevant parts. This requires an objectivity which, when dealing with people, may be difficult for him to apply rigorously. However, it is both to his benefit and to the benefit of the company, if it can be done.

'WHAT?'
This is the first question. What is happening at the present time? What forms are being used? What work is being done? What are the various files and records? What equipment is being used? And, finally, what are the staff levels in the departments? Having assessed this, the pathfinder then questions the people, examines the use of the equipment, and measures the activity of the staff. The initial enquiries about the company as a whole with regard to the forms and the work carried out make it possible to avoid a good deal of detailed questioning at this stage. It is not easy for the pathfinder to pick up a procedure and to gather all the data necessary from people and departments without having made some prior enquiry. This is due primarily to two factors: first, because it disrupts work, and, second, because of the sheer volume of data and the incapacity of the pathfinder to grasp this detail at one sitting.

'WHO?'

The facts gathered during questioning 'What?' are the basis of the next stage of the questioning sequence. This is the 'Who?' sequence. As previously stated, the reaction of departmental heads and section heads as to who does what vary, and the situation becomes even more confusing when discussing the detail with the clerks concerned. To ask who does the work is often reasonable and straightforward, but to ask who is responsible is a different matter altogether, and this is perhaps the key area for detailed consideration. This will be discussed later. Who requires data and to whom will the documents be sent? This again links with the original enquiry on activities.

The pathfinder should already have a reasonable idea of the work carried out by certain individuals, but only in a general sense. Now he collects more detailed information, remembering, of course, that he is tracing the path of a particular procedure and an individual may be involved in more than one specific procedure. This is where the objectivity of the pathfinder again comes into play.

'WHERE?'

The next series of questions concerns where the activities are carried out, and where people and machines are located. This deals with the problems of layout. The pathfinder must know the exact positions of departments, of people and equipment, including filing cabinets, shelves, bookcases, etc. This information will be used to analyse the layout of the offices which will be dealt with later.

'WHEN?'

This questioning sequence provides some of the most interesting information. If one starts to question when the work is done, a variety of answers are received from a variety of sources. Other questions which get varied responses are: 'When do peaks occur?' and 'When is overtime worked?' It is important to know when people consider activities should take place, and the pathfinder should attempt to formulate a timetable for the entire procedure. If he does this and records all the answers, he will find he has a very interesting timetable with many overlaps and discrepancies.

'HOW?'

How is the work done? How is it controlled? These two questions have to be considered and answered by the pathfinder in the light of his questioning and observations during the previous stages. If a clerk is asked how he does his job, it is doubtful whether he will know how to answer. The main method of gathering the facts for 'How?' is probably by observation. A skilled observer will be able to assess quickly how the work is done and to record this information in a way which will lead easily to further analysis.

SUMMARY

In each of the above sections several questions have been posed. These are not exhaustive; the pathfinder will need to ask other questions depending on circumstances. The aim at this stage is to establish exactly what is happening at the present time and to ensure that the following main questions have been covered:

What?
Who?
Where?
When?
How?

The path taken

The pathfinder should now have a sketch view of the procedure which forms a skeleton. This skeleton may also indicate certain problems and certain discrepancies which the pathfinder will find useful as the basis for the second stage, which is to establish the path taken by the present procedure. It is this next stage which leads directly to consideration of how the path may be improved. One of the interesting aspects which often emerges is that the pathfinder may find that he knows more about the procedure than any of the people involved in operating it. In particular this applies to departmental heads.

A recent example was a path I decided to follow in respect of the issue and charging of fuel used by a fleet of vehicles. Questioning the garage staff in respect of the recording of garage repair and maintenance costs and subsequent completion of vehicle performance records, it was discovered that the personnel in the garage office had nothing to do with the recording of fuel issues. This seemed to be somewhat questionable. Delving further it was established that the forms were sent over to the general office. It was not known to whom, so the general office staff were questioned. After several conflicting answers the clerk concerned was eventually found and questioned on how the sheets were used and what information was extracted.

The path meandered via a series of stages. Finally, the information was summarized by a punched card operator before punching for the accounting system and the subsequent charging out. It became apparent that part of the work was also being done from a copy by the clerk responsible for the driver's wages. In fact, on further examination, it was established that he was entering details of fuel on the daily work sheet from where it was extracted for the performance records. It was apparent that the information was being input into the system in two places, one of which could easily be eliminated. That analysis was left for the subsequent process.

'WHY?'

Having now established the basic path, the pathfinder must ask a further series of most vital questions. These questions are concerned with why things happen. At this stage the answers to the questions already asked must be looked at again and the question 'Why?' added. This will put the meat on the skeleton. On several occasions, I have been asked why this question is not asked at the same time as the pathfinder is gathering data in respect of the other questions. There is a simple answer. Earlier, the pathfinder is not in a position to be objective about this point. It is a question which has to be related to an understanding of the whole procedure. The pathfinder is not simply seeking an answer to an isolated question about detail. It is the answers to a series of whys. He must continually be able to point the question in the direction that he wishes to take. If the pathfinder simply asks, 'Why do you do it like that?' the answer might well be, 'Because the supervisor told me to do it like that'. Now obviously that begs the question; it is not an answer which is of any use to the pathfinder.

One of the most annoying forms of question is the continuous 'Why?' question. When it is asked the first time and an incomplete answer is received, the question is repeated until a complete answer *is* received. By this process the pathfinder is not necessarily seeking to find the errors or omissions in the procedures, but to get a complete picture of the process. He is not really in a position to judge at this stage whether the answers he receives are correct or not, although he may already have seen some glaring examples of wasteful effort, so he must not prejudge his final analysis of the situation. For the moment, he must be objective in obtaining the answers to his questions and in completing any apparent gaps in the data he has collected and recorded. It is his ability to record in a logical form the answers to his questions which enable him to make a sound judgement later.

Recording the path

With skill and good fortune the pathfinder gets answers to most of his questions, and, during the course of his questioning, will have recorded the pertinent points raised. Recording is not as easy as it may at first appear. It is not only rude, but it is difficult to simply write down everything. It is impossible to listen attentively and record accurately at the same time. Therefore, the pathfinder must learn how to record key points and how to fill in the lesser facts from memory. Using the form detail sheet and the activity analysis completed in the initial enquiry, he can complete his questioning and prepare full records of the answers received. From these answers, the pathfinder begins to see the direction of the path. This is done by drawing out a procedure narrative (Fig. 4.2) which is the record of

DEPARTMENT	ACTIVITY	DOCUMENT

Fig. 4.2   Procedure narrative

each step of the procedure as it takes place, using an analysis of the answers to the questions. This procedure narrative is concerned with detailing each activity within the procedure. An example of a procedure narrative would be as follows:

Step 1   Determine the requirement for parts by examining the shelf on which the parts normally reside

Step 2   Complete an order requisition in duplicate, entering the date, description of the parts, part number and the stores location/number

Step 3   Send the top copy of the order requisition to the buying department, file the second copy in the stores department

Step 4   Buying department reference the order requisition to the buying record and extract details of supplier, which are then entered on the order requisition

Step 5   Make out an official order in triplicate

Step 6   Send the top copy of the order set to the supplier

Step 7   Send the second copy to the stores

Step 8   File the third copy of the order in the supplier's outstanding order file

Step 9   Stores will receive the copy order and enter on the stores requisition

Step 10   File the stores requisition and the copy order in the outstanding order file.

The above narrative is simple and straightforward and indicates the path being followed in placing an order. The key points in the procedure are the activities which take place, where they take place and their purpose. Something a little more detailed than the procedure narrative is needed before the path can be established. The additional record is known as the information flow and this is dealt with by preparing a chart as shown in Fig. 4.3.

This chart is still in narrative form. It is subsequently used to create the detailed procedure flowchart which provides a pictorial presentation of the path followed by the procedures. Recording the procedure leads the pathfinder to the gaps; a lack of flow indicates an unanswered question or misinterpretation of the information which has been collected. It is dangerous when recording information always to assume that the person providing the answer is at fault. Frequently, the questioner may misinterpret or misunderstand the answers. Great care must be taken when completing gaps that

STORES	BUYER	SUPPLIER
① Determine requirements		
② Prepare Order Requisition		
③ Send Order Requisition →	→ ④ Receive Order	
⑤ File copy Order	Requisition	
Requisition	⑥ Code reference and	
	establish who to buy from	
	⑦ Prepare Official Order	
⑨ Receive copy order ←	← ⑧ Distribute order →	→
⑩ Enter Order No. onto		
Order Requisition		
⑪ File Order Requisition	⑫ File Copy Order in the	
and Copy Order in the	Outstanding Order file	
outstanding file		

Fig. 4.3   Information flow

responsibility is always taken by the questioner. Comments such as, 'I've misunderstood what you said', or 'I'm afraid I forgot to ask you about this', are appreciated by the staff because there is no blame attached to them. It is clear that the questioner is fallible, and this is always a good point to press home.

It must be stressed that the recording of facts is absolutely vital to every stage which follows. Not only is the pathfinder establishing the path followed by the procedure, the forms used, the activities and the location, etc., but he is also recording such things as duplications in the system, problems experienced, opinions and attitudes, all of which help to decide upon an improved procedure. The flowcharts which are used in analysis are entirely constructed from the information that has been collected during the questioning process. Unless this has been properly recorded, it is virtually impossible to prepare accurate charts.

The records may also contain many suggestions and ideas from the staff which could be of value when the new procedures are being developed. It is imperative that the ideas and suggestions offered are seen to be recorded by the pathfinder. Probably the best approach is always to have a note book or a sheet of paper which is clearly headed 'Staff suggestions and ideas for the development of new procedures', so that when any idea is proposed it can be seen to be written on this sheet. Much mistrust may arise if the pathfinder does not make it clear that he is not going to take the credit for anybody else's ideas and suggestions. If the improved procedures are successful, then the general credit, of course, belongs to the pathfinder himself. It is true to say, however, that the procedure which is easiest to sell is the one to which the manager feels he has contributed. In other words, it is not necessary to sell a man his own idea.

The principal record leading to effective analysis of procedure and clerical activities is undoubtedly the procedure flowchart. Several different forms of this have been developed from work-study techniques of long-standing. However, these techniques are not particularly applicable to the recording and charting of clerical procedures, so the pathfinder should use any form of charting which he finds effective. No particular form of charting is any better than another, and in Appendix 1 a variety of such systems is shown. The one which is suggested here as particularly appropriate to clerical activities is the general flowchart which has been named 'information and document flowchart' (see Appendix 2). Before examining the use of this method in more detail perhaps it is worth while to consider the main reasons why charts are of value and some of the principals involved in using them effectively. The reasons for using charts can be listed as follows:

1. They enforce the consideration of each step in logical sequence
2. They indicate any missing steps
3. They indicate the deficiencies of the information and document flow, and apparent duplications

4. They eliminate the variable interpretation that can be placed upon words
5. They clearly show the path which the procedure follows, on one piece of paper.

If any procedure chart takes up more than can be reasonably drawn on one sheet of paper, it must be subdivided into manageable sections. One of the greatest advantages of charts is that they make available a means of managing a vast amount of information which can be collected from some of the more complex procedures. A series of five or six information and document flowcharts can be much easier to analyse and interpret than fifteen or twenty pages of procedure narrative. One of the main principles of charting is the use of symbols in place of words. The information and document flowchart suggested in this chapter as being the most appropriate, uses both symbols and words as relevant. Many of the charting systems which are available (see Appendix 1) cannot be as easily

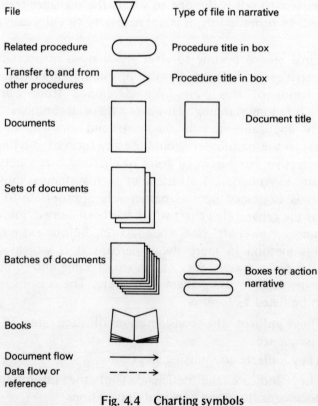

Fig. 4.4   Charting symbols

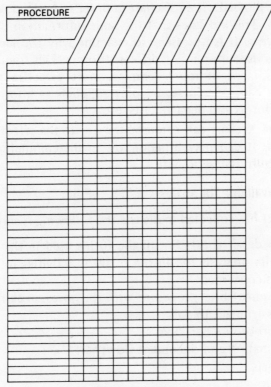

PROCEDURE

Fig. 4.5   X chart

interpreted as one which uses a few words in the right place; the lack
of them means cross-referencing to a procedure narrative, to obtain a
full and accurate picture.

For the sake of clarity symbols used in the drawing of information
and document flowcharts are shown in Fig. 4.4. When drawing charts
of procedures concerned with computer applications, the generally
accepted symbols for systems charts as shown in Appendix 1, page
141 should be used. This avoids confusion between the symbols used
for charting clerical activities and those used for charting computer
systems. It does not generally take long to develop the knack of
using charts effectively, provided that one is not hide-bound by
conventions and is able to make use of symbols and methods
developed by oneself in order to deal with a particular problem or
pictorial message.

In addition to the information and document flowchart, it is often
necessary to use the X chart (Fig. 4.5). The value of the X chart is in
relating two factors together. The information and the forms in a

procedure are plotted on an X chart in order to break down the data being handled. This indicates that the same information is being used on several forms. It is necessary to examine why the same piece of information is used in so many different forms. This frequently leads to the development of much simpler, more effective procedures. Other factors can, of course, be plotted, such as information and departments, forms and departments, etc.

The use of the X chart can often be the key to the effective revision of procedures. It can play a major role in the elimination of many wasteful and purposeless activities.

Information available for analysis

The pathfinder has collected in his file the following records:

1. Form detail sheets for all the forms used in the procedures
2. Activity analysis for all the relevant activities in the departments concerned
3. Assignment brief, together with the notes on carrying out of the assignment to date
4. The procedure narrative
5. Information and document flowchart
6. X charts.

Now, a further extremely important record has to be prepared. This is known as the interaction chart and simply sets down the related procedures which are affected by the procedure under examination. Although these are not being looked at in detail at this stage, it is important that this interaction chart is prepared and examined. When revised procedures are being developed the pathfinder can make sure that any interaction with other procedures is fully catered for and that there is no lack of information due to oversight of any related activities.

An example of a simple procedure has been given in Appendix 2 with full details of all the above records clearly shown. From this example, the reader may easily understand why the logical questioning and recording processes are so essential to effective design of good systems. This is one of the prime requirements for the successful control of paperwork.

5 Finding a better path

In trying to improve the present procedures, the pathfinder should follow a sequence of three steps using the information which he has collected.

1. Analysis
2. Establishing the problem
3. Developing alternative solutions.

Throughout this stage of the overall assignment, the need for objectivity must be paramount. There are always some solutions which present themselves as obvious answers to the problem, but the objectivity of the pathfinder should help him to develop the possibilities without this bias.

Analysis

Using the records and charts created during the questioning processes, the pathfinder should proceed to analyse his information in order to identify those parts of the procedures which require attention. Many procedures achieve the purpose for which they were established, but may have become rather cumbersome and can therefore often be improved.

However, it is sometimes necessary to design a completely new procedure based on a clear identification of the problem. This complete building of a new system should not be the pathfinder's first approach. Such drastic action is not often necessary. Frequently the existing procedures can be suitably amended with considerable savings and additional benefits and with the minimum of change.

In order to decide whether the procedures should be amended or completely renewed the pathfinder has to examine his information very carefully. In doing this he is looking for the following areas upon which he will take action.

1. Key activities

When examining the document and information flowchart and the other records that have been collected, the pathfinder is concerned to identify those activities which are the basis for the success of the procedure. They may be numerous, but it should be established whether, if this activity was removed, a major problem would arise.

2. Secondary activities

If an activity is not considered to be of primary importance, it may nevertheless have some value and may then be classified as a secondary activity. This is an activity which, if removed, would require an alternative operation to be carried out.

3. Unnecessary activities

These activities are identified when the previous two sections have been dealt with, for all activities which are neither key activities nor secondary activities can be considered unnecessary, and should be eliminated.

4. Poor workflow

This is apparent when the work appears to be moving frequently between departments with little if any direction or effective use of information. It will be necessary to consider a change in workflow when activities have been properly classified.

5. Surplus documents

One of the main advantages of the information and document flowchart is the way in which it clearly indicates documentation which does not appear to have any particular purpose. It may be surplus copies of a necessary document or complete documents themselves which are unnecessary. They will appear to be surplus because they will not be used by the key activities. If this is not the case, then their purpose must be carefully questioned. Reference to the records of documents, activities and procedure narratives will help identify surplus documents.

6. Duplication of effort

This is probably the one area in clerical activities which is the most obvious when carrying out analysis and yet it is one of the most difficult to remove. Duplication of effort is often hidden by the way different activities are described. They may be described as 'checking' or 'recording', but if they are apparently carrying out the same work, albeit in a slightly different way, then it is most certainly duplication of effort. Again, from the records which have been collected, the pathfinder is able to identify clerical operations which he considers to be a duplication. Further information may be needed before he can decide which can be eliminated.

7. *Superfluous information*

This is an area which leads to much disagreement. What is essential may be a matter of opinion. To one manager a particular piece of information is vital. To another manager it is of no use whatsoever. It is this discrepancy of managerial approach which causes many unnecessary problems in clerical procedures. It is often necessary to provide both pieces of information usually from the same basic data. In analysing the procedure and the activities, this problem has to be dealt with by establishing what information is needed. Without this it is difficult to consider how to design new and improved procedures. There is no easy answer, and managers frequently state that they do not know what information they want and ask for as much information as possible. They even suggest that the office manager should decide the information that they need.

This processing and analysing of the facts and figures which have been collected is a very important process. When the seven stages of analysis have been carried out, it will be necessary for the pathfinder to return to ask more questions. These additional questions will be primarily concerned with establishing whether activities, documents, effort and information are necessary and who considers them so. These additional questions are all part of the analysis process and from these questions and the answers received the pathfinder will develop his system specification. The system specification is a document which sets down the purposes of the system, the key activities, the key documents and the principal areas of clerical effort. Finally, but most important, it will lay down the information required by the user at the end of the system.

The system specification (Fig. 5.1) is different from the assignment brief in that it is an attempt to lay down the precise requirements for the revised or the new system. It is during this process of analysis and problem identification that the pathfinder is able to establish clearly the system specification. As will be seen later in this chapter, without this specification it becomes almost impossible to develop suitable alternatives for management consideration. Unless alternatives are compared using a carefully designed specification then it will be extremely difficult to make correct decisions about the best systems to adopt.

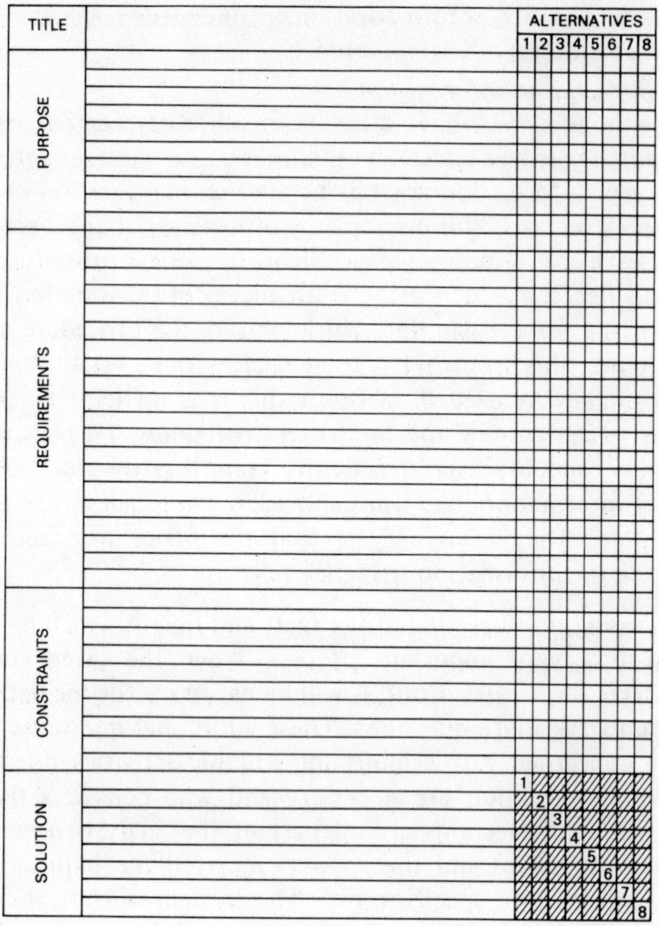

Fig. 5.1 System specification

Establishing the problem

Finding the problem is not as easy as it may appear. When the information has been collected it is desirable to return to the initial problems to check if they are the real ones. In some cases, the apparent problems associated with documentation and activities can be identified as a matter of human relations, or the management and operation of the procedure itself. Dealing with human relations is not easy and calls for a tactful and purposeful approach.

The pathfinder must at this stage of his investigation be clear as to where the problems lie. It is of little value to examine in depth any alternative approaches unless he has identified the real problems. This involves the analysis of opinion rather than fact and is difficult. It also involves the subjective evaluation of the opinions of different individuals and their prejudices, and calls for much diplomacy.

An assignment was called for in a medium-sized engineering company which manufactured large machines on a small-batch basis. The problem was stated to be that the stores control procedures were not operating properly. They were failing to provide an effective service to the factory; the works manager was having difficulty in meeting the delivery schedule because parts were not available when required.

The purpose of the assignment was to establish an effective stock control procedure which would ensure timely ordering of parts to avoid production delays. The assignment got under way. A good deal of information was collected with regard to stores procedures. During the analysis of this information it transpired that, from the store manager's point of view, the principal problem was notification from the works of what was wanted and when.

It seemed logical that if these requirements were not notified in sufficient time, the stores would have difficulty in ordering. However, the works manager stated quite categorically that as soon as an order was received and drawings had been prepared, a complete breakdown of parts was passed to the stores for action. The whole problem associated with the lack of parts in stock seemed to derive from this key activity, one for which neither of the two managers concerned accepted any responsibility. The works manager notified the stores manager as soon as he was aware of the parts required. The stores manager in his turn ordered these parts as soon as he received notification. The question was why were the parts not available when required. After considerable discussion with the managers concerned, and with the drawing office and order department, it was established that for many parts the delivery time from the supplier was considerably longer than the time it took to manufacture the finished machine, if all parts were available. It was not difficult to identify the parts which were causing the problem. The system was changed so that the delivery scheduling to customers was based on availability of parts rather than the capacity of the factory. This correct identification of the problem led to a speedy and satisfactory solution without the design of a new procedure.

The pathfinder must ask himself the following questions: What is the real problem? Is it the system? Is it the environment in which the system operates, or is it the people who operate the system? He must go further and try to establish what the system is trying to achieve. From here he can move to the specification of the system required. In the example given above it is apparent that the only change necessary was to change the way in which the procedure was operated. A small change, but one of major significance. It is surprising how often this type of amendment to procedures can considerably improve their effectiveness.

Until the pathfinder can identify where the problem lies, he cannot effectively direct his attention to its solution. Misdirection is a vital consideration when faced with a very broad area with many possible approaches. The time and effort which can be spent in finding the solution is considerable. If the problems can be precisely assessed, this time can be shortened and the solution can be much more effective. Unfortunately it is not always possible to make this assessment, however essential this may be. In many cases, the conflicting opinions of management leave the pathfinder himself to state the problem. On his skill in doing this may depend the design of successful and efficient systems.

When seeking answers to the above questions, the pathfinder must first check the records he has created in the preceding stages of the assignment. If the system itself seems sound, with little or no unnecessary activities, no duplication, no surplus documents, then the pathfinder must look towards the environment and the circumstances in which the procedure operates. These may be the physical environment or the rules and constraints within which the procedure operates. If these seem logical and practical and do not offer any obstacles to effective working, then the pathfinder must look to the people involved and must try to establish where the system is failing and who is responsible. This can be an unpleasant part of the process and can lead to a good deal of dissension among, and poor relations with, the people involved. However, a new system may not overcome a personality problem. Treating symptoms is never a cure for the disease.

System specification

Having analysed the facts and figures and having established the problem, the pathfinder now moves to setting down the detailed system specification in a format as is shown in Fig. 5.1. The analysis and problem-finding stages, together with the resultant system specification, are shown in Appendix 3, which, if used with the data recorded in Appendix 2, provide a direct detailed example of the operation of the previous stages in the overall process of controlling paperwork. Looking at the systems specification and following the main headings it can be seen that a list of requirements is being formulated against which all alternative solutions must be matched before they can be accepted as viable alternatives.

The requirements are set out in three sections:

1. Purpose
2. Requirements
3. Constraints.

PURPOSE

Purpose covers why that system is necessary. It does not deal with a variety of functions carried out by the system, but the main reason for the system. An example of this would be a purchase accounting system which normally has two aims: first, the timely and accurate payment to the supplier, and, second, the analysis of accounting information. The purpose has to be clearly understood. Many systems have an apparent purpose which on examination is found to be entirely different.

REQUIREMENTS

Requirements of the system will be the criteria. These may be quite extensive in some procedures and may be met by using alternatives. The alternatives will be matched against the purpose and requirements and will be discarded if they don't meet the systems specification. It is imperative, therefore, that the requirements are listed fully and accurately. Otherwise valid alternatives may be discarded.

CONSTRAINTS

It is rarely possible to develop systems which do not have any constraints either in the form of organization, company policy, money available for equipment, manpower, etc. The constraints must be noted and attention given to them when matching the alternatives against the specification. Examples of purpose and requirements can be seen on the systems specification in Appendix 3.

Developing alternatives

When the systems specification has been prepared it is proper to consider alternatives. This is done by a further questioning routine which examines the answers given in the initial stages, i.e., answers in respect of how the system is operated, where it is done, etc., and asks the following questions.

How else can it be done?
Where else can it be done?
What else can be done?
Can it be done at any other time?
Who else can do it?

The replies to these questions may be many, and the pathfinder will need skill to establish feasible alternatives. No clear-cut solutions may present themselves, but if the pathfinder has done his job well, many ideas and opinions will be expressed by both management and staff, and these ideas and opinions, together with the answers to the questions, should lead him to at least two or three alternatives.

The need for alternatives is often questioned. Why is it not possible to go directly to the new and revised procedures? The reason is that the range of possibilities in designing systems from the documentation, the staffing and equipment layout, etc., are considerable. Variables are great, and even within a tight set of constraints, it is possible to vary the system in many ways from the cheap system to the expensive system. It is desirable when developing these alternatives to offer management a choice as to approach, method and operation. Indeed, if the pathfinder is to be objective, he must consider all possibilities rather than decide at an early stage on one particular answer which may not necessarily be the best. Objectivity is not an attribute which is easily acquired, and it is this process of examining alternatives which helps towards it.

When a suitable number of alternatives have been assessed, at this stage in principle only, they can be graded according to the following scale: probables, possibles and doubtfuls. The next steps in selecting the appropriate alternative will be a series of eliminating questions, based on matching the alternatives against the systems specification. As each alternative is checked against the specification, it is discarded until only those which are valid remain. Using the basic rule that the simplest is best, a further analysis can be carried out in order to assess which of the valid alternatives is the simplest to operate.

Reference to the example in Appendix 3 will show how several alternatives have been developed in principle and have been checked off against the system specification. Then the flowcharts for each alternative should be examined in order to arrive at the simplest procedure which will achieve the purpose and meet all the requirements of the systems specification.

Reviewing

The pathfinder is about to change his role from one of gathering information and of developing ideas to one with a more artistic flavour, namely, the design of the selected system. However, before he moves into this role it is necessary to review the steps at present taken in order to assess how he should develop the solution. It is possible when looking at this kind of assignment to develop the solution in four main ways.

1. The structure can be reorganized
2. A new system can be designed
3. The existing system can be modified
4. Within the existing system, methods and equipment can be changed.

Whichever of these four approaches is taken, it is necessary to discuss it in detail with the management concerned and to obtain their approval. The different approaches listed above clearly have a different impact on different departments. Looking at the list the impact is reduced as we descend the list. Reorganization is the approach with the greatest impact and changing the methods is the approach with the least impact. If an effective solution is to be developed, the right approach must be selected. The alternatives which have so far been developed will be further reduced if the management select an approach which is completely different.

The processes outlined in this chapter have taken the assignment from the collection of information through to the development of alternative solutions and the desired approach in developing the answer. These steps are extremely important and any lack of effort in carrying them out will be shown up in the quality of the solution to the problem. It is not an easy process, this process of analysis and questioning for alternatives. It is one of the most difficult processes in the whole development of good systems and a great deal of time and effort must be devoted to it. The example in Appendix 3 shows how the facts gathered and the flowcharts that have been drawn can lead to the development of a variety of alternatives. When these have been checked and the approach agreed, the final selection of the most appropriate alternative can be made.

The next stage is the detailed development of this alternative into an accepted system covering all aspects of the procedures, staffing, equipment, etc. This has to be done in great detail and requires great thoroughness on the part of the individual carrying out the assignment.

The next chapter will deal with designing the system, documents, etc. This is a more artistic role for the pathfinder and provides an opportunity to use flair and imagination.

6 Artist at work

Designing new systems calls for a good deal of creativity as well as a logical mind. Although both attributes are desirable, the principal requirement of a logical objective approach is essential. When designing new procedures the systems designer has to bear in mind all the information which has been collected and be able to base his design on the alternative approach to the problem which he has chosen. The design of an effective system requires making decisions about questions asked previously: What is to be done? How is it to be done? Where is it to be carried out? By whom is it to be carried out? When is it to be carried out?

These five questions have been answered in respect of the existing procedures and have also been examined in the light of the alternative methods available. The systems designer must use this information to determine the most efficient and effective solutions within the alternative approach selected. This calls for critical examination of the factors involved in the system to be designed. The starting point is the requirements of the procedure as clearly stated in the systems specification and it must be ensured that these requirements are fully achieved. The examination of alternatives will have already indicated that the chosen one is feasible. The detailed design has not yet been established and when it has it is quite possible that the details may conflict overall with how the chosen alternative should operate. Many additional problems can arise which have not been encountered in developing the alternative.

The problems of systems designers can be overcome if the following rules are used as a basis.

1. Ensure the purpose is achieved
2. Use the minimum of clerical effort
3. Permit no peaks in the workflow
4. Ensure a smooth flow of data
5. Make all required information available for each activity
6. Permit a minimum of data handling

7. Limit the amount of checking to the minimum desirable
8. Permit as few documents as possible
9. File reference as little as possible
10. Try to cater for exceptions.

What is to be done

The systems specification lays down the requirements of the system. This is interpreted by the systems designer into the principal activities required. These activities have already been analysed and certain degrees of priority have been laid down. The systems designer must ensure that these activities fall within the rules outlined above and that they are vital to the system. When the activities have been established, the systems designer is in a position to consider the methods he should use to ensure these activities are linked together in a smooth, effective working pattern. Often, too little attention is given to this first stage. Frequently the requirements of a system appear to be obvious and to require little detailed attention. It is desirable to ensure that the requirements are valid. If this is not clearly established now, then the systems designer must go over this ground again in order to ensure that he is not designing a system which is not required. Critical examination must be made over and over again. If the systems requirements are examined at each stage of development, then, at the conclusion, there will be no doubt that they will have been proved to be really necessary.

How to achieve the requirements

The methods to be used have already been considered in principle. It is now the job of the systems designer to develop these methods in detail and to examine the forms and equipment required; he must also decide the data to be employed within the system. This development is one of the most intricate activities undertaken by the systems designer: he must be thorough to the extreme of being pedantic. The principles of form design and selection of equipment will be dealt with more fully at the end of this chapter. In considering methods, the systems designer should use flowcharts and the various products of equipment manufacturers. Information which is vital to the design of systems should have already been collected. This covers the volumes of data and documents which at present flow through the system, the timing of the receipt of such data, the time when the information is required, the duties of existing personnel, etc. All this information should be available to the systems designer, so that he can ensure that the methods he is developing are capable of handling the volumes and meeting the times required.

The systems designer will need to discuss the methods under examination with management. He should also assess the relative cost of different methods. It might appear that working within a chosen alternative approach the number of methods is limited. This is true to some extent, but the imaginative systems designer should be able to produce a variety of methods from which an optimum method will have to be chosen. The systems designer should be able to make some of the selections himself, but there is no point in developing a system which management will not accept because it does not cater for local circumstances or management preferences, so the management must be involved in the decision.

A systems designer working on a new stores procedure had arrived at two possible methods of recording goods received. These were:

1. A daily goods received sheet
2. An individual goods received note.

The stores management preferred the daily goods received sheet which required less preparation and was an easier document to use when recording details of receipt on the stock records. The accounts department preferred the individual goods received note because these could be filed alphabetically to await the suppliers' invoices. The systems designer established that the benefits of each method were equivalent, but were achieved in the different departments, i.e., the goods received sheet was better for the stores, but the goods received note was better for the accounts. There was no clear-cut benefit upon which this decision could be made. It therefore had to be made by management. Having due regard to pressure of work, management decided that the goods received note would suit them better.

The involvement of management in this kind of decision is vital if the eventual system is to be accepted and implemented. Management often look unfavourably at a system which has been designed without their involvement. This is known as the 'systems designer's system'. The problem with such a system is that if difficulties are encountered or if the system fails, management can disclaim any responsibility. It is therefore to the benefit of the systems designer to involve them at every point where disagreement is likely to be encountered, even where selection of detailed methods has little overall effect on the system to be designed. If the systems designer is convinced that one particular method is better than another, he must ensure that he can prove his conviction. This is where the designer's objectivity should prevail.

The location of the activities

In selecting the most appropriate place for work to be done, the systems designer is determining to a large extent the efficiency of the new system. It is common to encounter a system where work can be carried out in many locations. In selecting the most appropriate location, the systems designer must have regard to the relative costs and effectiveness of each possible location and also to some degree upon managements' preference. One decision which always has to be made is whether to centralize or whether to decentralize activities. The systems designer must consider this decision only in the light of what is appropriate in each particular case: centralization may be as beneficial as decentralization. The circumstances and environment are the deciding factors every time this question is raised. The systems designer must clearly establish which location is best.

In any system there are logical points where the handling of data meets what could be termed as a 'natural break'. This is one of the points where the transmission of data from one location to another should take place. It is only in this way that additional handling and duplication of effort can be avoided. Searching for natural breaks in data handling procedures becomes second nature to the experienced systems designer, and there is little doubt that this is one of his most important and beneficial roles.

In a large company, with several operating areas, the purchasing procedure was operated in two locations. The local offices ordered their requirements from the suppliers and received the invoices for those supplies. These invoices were checked for receipt of the goods or services and then passed to head office to be coded by supplier, analysed and entered on input sheets for computer processing. This operation did not achieve the desired results. Invoices were mislaid and often processed twice. Suppliers' queries were many and varied and sometimes could not be handled at either the local or the central office. This often meant enquiries at both locations before a satisfactory answer could be found.

The system was examined and a revised procedure instituted. This changed the point where work was carried out so that a natural break was used to transmit the data from one location to another. This natural break came at the point where the data was prepared for computer input. All the work prior to this was carried out at the area office. The goods were checked for receipt, invoices were coded, analysis codes entered and the information was then put on computer input sheets at the area offices for transmission to the computer.

The effect of this was considerable. Less staff were required. Less suppliers' queries were received and those that were received were more effectively handled. Less documents were mislaid and very few, if any, invoices were processed twice. The reasons for this are partly obvious, but one of the most important factors was hidden; this was that the processing of data should be carried out as near to the point where the data was created. At this point the greatest knowledge is available about the data concerned. This was almost certainly the most important factor in the decision to locate this procedure at the area offices and to use the principle of finding a natural break. The result was a great improvement.

One further point in deciding the location is the ability of the personnel to carry out these activities. If personnel are not employed primarily for clerical purposes, then the burden of clerical activity placed upon them should be kept to a minimum. This can lead directly to a decision about the most appropriate location. Having decided the location the next stage is to establish who should carry out the work.

Who is to carry out the work?

The systems designer has available the information about the personnel located at each point and can assess who should do the various jobs. When he has decided this, he should then obtain the agreement of management. This will establish whether the grading and responsibility of the personnel meet with the work requirements of each activity. This part of overall procedure design is vital when it comes to determining the staffing levels and obtaining management agreement to the new system. There has to be a balance between the work content of a job and the person's ability to do the job, though one would not totally disregard the ability of the individual. To do so would nearly always mean a change of personnel. This is not the function of the systems designer. His function is to ensure that the system and work within that system is carried out effectively. It is a management decision to select personnel to carry out the work. They must therefore be closely involved in arriving at this balance between work content and staff suitability. If the systems designer oversteps this critical line and proceeds to suggest the most appropriate personnel, he will encounter a good deal of management resistance. Determining the staff levels, i.e., numbers of staff required, will be covered in the next chapter on Introducing Change. It is the systems designer's job to assess the amount of work and to put this before management so that they can clearly see the overall effects of the staff.

When is the work to be done?

The timing of activities will fall into a pattern once the previous parts of the systems have been decided upon. The input of data from sources within or from outside the company will determine to a large extent the frequency of activities. The systems designer must develop his system to ensure that activities are clearly marked as to whether they are to be done daily, weekly, monthly, etc. In doing this he must bear in mind all that has gone before and particularly avoid peak working conditions, which is often difficult.

There are many factors contributing to peaking of work which are outside the control of the individuals concerned. One example of this is the work of the mail department, which clearly has a peak in the morning and in the evening. These peaks cannot be completely avoided because there are only a certain number of postal deliveries and collections. Wherever peak work can be avoided, then the timing of activities should be arranged to ensure that spreading takes place. Once again it will depend largely upon circumstances and must be very carefully considered. The systems designer is in the best position to carry out this examination and to ensure that his timings cover the volumes and the requirements of the system. Then he must discuss the timing of the work with management to obtain agreement about the resultant effect on staffing levels and the flow of data.

The timing of related activities is one of the most important areas in clerical procedures and has a significant effect on efficiency of methods and people. If one factor alone had to be selected as the reason why clerical procedures were inefficient, this might well be that one.

Selling the new system

The systems designer should by now have completed the design of the new system. It will not yet be ready for implementation, but most of the rough edges should have been smoothed out. He should have available his flowchart, the forms required, lists of the activities, where they are to be carried out and the people concerned. He should also have a timing schedule of the activities. From this he will develop his approach to management in order to obtain agreement about details. Agreement should be sought at two levels: first, with the operating staff, and, second, with management. It should be done in this order because if the operating staff agree with the details then they will support it in discussion with management.

There are three ways in which a new system can be explained to management:

1. Reporting
2. Discussion
3. Presentation and demonstration.

The selection of the method to be used will depend on the circumstances, the people involved and the complexity of the system concerned. The systems designer must make this selection very carefully indeed.

REPORTS

Written reports are perhaps the most frequently used method of presenting new systems to management, and to use it successfully the systems designer should develop an ability for the preparation of reports and for their presentation. Writing reports is not a simple process. It is necessary to write clearly and concisely and to present arguments in such a way that the reader fully understands the writer's thoughts and so ensure an understanding of the processes leading to his recommendations. The report writer cannot report all the data and information which has been collected throughout the assignment. He must therefore be able to summarize the information in a form which allows for a full appreciation of the subject matter.

It is as well for the report writer to practise what he preaches: the point has already been made that management have enough information to absorb without now receiving more paperwork.

In order to present the subject as succinctly as possible, but also to provide enough information, the report writer should follow a prescribed pattern. I have used the following method of report writing successfully for many years:

1. Title page which will contain the date, the subject matter and the distribution of the report
2. An introduction to the subject matter
3. A summary of recommendations
4. An abbreviation of the present methods used
5. Scope of the survey
6. Observations on recommendations
7. Appendices.

Introduction

The introduction should detail the reason why the survey has been carried out, who asked for the survey to be done and the ultimate aim.

Summary of recommendations

Each recommendation should be written briefly and clearly so that there is no doubt whatsoever about the suggestion being made. The recommendations should be short and simply state facts. The following are examples of concise recommendations:

1. That a visible record computer be introduced
2. That the following systems are processed on the said visible record computer:
   (a) Sales
   (b) Purchases
   (c) Accounts
   (d) Payroll
3. That the staff in the accounts department be reduced
4. The visible record computer be introduced within six months
5. That the wages, cashiers, purchase, sales and invoicing departments be amalgamated.

The aim of summarizing recommendations is to enable the reader to obtain a speedy grasp of the subject matter and to be able to read the remainder of the report on the basis of justifying the recommendations.

Present method

The report writer should present this as briefly as possible indicating the salient points and the problems which were found to exist. Inserting this in the report enables the reader to focus on the reason for recommendations.

Scope of survey

This is the section in which the report writer should describe clearly the work in the survey and enable the reader to see that the recommendations have been made after due consideration. Again, this should be a fairly brief section which should show what work has been done and the timetable followed.

Observation on recommendation

In this section each recommendation and the reason for it are dealt with separately and fully, and a considerable amount of time should be spent on it. This section should form the basis of his arguments for each recommendation. Each observation should repeat the recommendation and, wherever possible, indicate that the recommendation has been arrived at with the agreement of management. This is perhaps the most important section of the report and provides the opportunity for the writer to present a clearly argued case for his recommendations.

Appendices

Appendices are extremely useful in removing detailed statistics, tables, volumes, times, etc., from the body of the report. If this is done, the body of the report will be much more readable, but there should be a cross-reference in the text to the relevant parts of the appendices. This has to be done bearing in mind the length and complexity of the report. If it is a brief report, then appendices will not be required. If it is a complex report then appendices can be effective. It is very important to number the sections of the report. The best method is the decimal system used in Appendix 6.

Reports have certain advantages and disadvantages as follows:

Disadvantages. First, the reader may well consider a heavy report to be tedious. Second, it is not possible in a report to indicate the emphasis on the words used, which can cause misinterpretation or misunderstanding. This is perhaps one of the worst problems of writing a report. Third, a report generally challenges a reply when sent to a manager closely concerned with the recommendations and he may feel a need to reply in writing which can delay in reaching agreement.

Advantages. First, reports in a written form can be copied and sent to several people which gives them a wide circulation. Second, it is possible, using the above pattern, to present a logical, well-argued explanation for recommendations. Third, a report is always a considerable advantage to discussion and helps the early conclusion of an agreement.

DISCUSSION

When discussion with management takes place, it is important for the systems designer to control the course of the talks. His aim is to achieve agreement and this cannot be done when talks are uncontrolled. Formal meetings have to be carefully planned if they are to achieve anything. In planning talks the systems designer should have regard to the following points:

1. A general outline of the recommendations should be available. This can be in an abbreviated report as indicated above

2. It is emphasized that the recommendations should achieve the requirements of the system as laid down in the specifications previously agreed

3. The systems designer should avoid criticizing existing procedures and should merely point out the problem areas and how the recommended approach will overcome these

4. It is unnecessary to conceal any possible difficulties within the new system. The management concerned will readily see these and if the systems designer admits there are problems and solicits managements' support in overcoming them, then several steps have been taken towards achieving agreement

5. The discussion should be carefully planned and each step that the designer wants to achieve should be written down

6. It is vital for the systems designer to keep control of the discussion and not to allow speakers to digress unnecessarily

7. It is advisable for the systems designer to ask the managers present for their suggestions and ideas to improve the recommendations.

Discussion without a report has a marked disadvantage: it is lacking in purpose. It is not always possible in talk to make the same logical and forceful points which can be placed in a report. The spoken word is of great value in emphasizing particular aspects, but statistics cannot be effectively considered nor can the full effect of a complex topic be appreciated only by listening. It has been said that two-thirds of what one hears is not registered by the brain. Because of this, unless they are well-organized, discussions may fail to achieve their purpose.

PRESENTATION AND DEMONSTRATION

An old Chinese proverb states that one picture is worth a thousand words. This makes sense. There is no doubt that a well-drawn diagram or chart can show much more easily the process to be followed than can the spoken or written word. Presentation by diagram combines discussion and written report. It aims to provide in a visual and spoken manner the advantages of both.

It is vital for the systems designer to prepare a presentation very carefully. This is necessary because the whole point of the presentation is to take the listener through a carefully planned series of steps to achieve agreement to the recommendations. It is a good idea to write a report and to use this as the basis of the presentation and to make use of whatever facilities are available. Here are some of the more important types of visual aid which can be used.

1. An overhead projector enables the person making the presentation to produce on the screen an enlarged diagram or flowchart. In addition, he can also project on the screen the main points of his argument; this will draw the listeners' attention to those particular points
2. A blackboard
3. A flipchart which allows the presentation to be prepared in advance and for page by page presentation of facts and figures
4. Slide projectors, provided the slides are relevant and have been specially prepared
5. Films, again, provided they are relevant to the topics under discussion
6. Models, if specially made for the purpose, can be very effective in showing a particular aspect of the topic.

The following pointers will help any individual who is proposing to make a presentation of a new system or new method of approach.

1. Be humble and patient with the audience
2. Reiterate the agreed requirements of the system
3. Don't be hesitant in dealing with questions, and admit honestly if the answer is not known
4. Sell at the lowest level first. Don't present to top management if the middle and junior management have not seen and appreciated the presentation
5. Be ready to compromise if obvious advantageous suggestions are made by the audience. Avoid being dogmatic
6. Prepare the balance sheet of pros and cons
7. Be cautious of trial runs of the system which may well be suggested by the audience. There is no need for a trial run if agreement can be reached without it
8. Avoid using jargon
9. Take pains to prepare good charts and diagrams
10. Lobby for support prior to the presentation
11. Relate savings to profits. Ensure that all savings or benefits indicated within the recommendations do add to the profits
12. Rehearse the presentation and amend any areas which appear to fall flat.

Perhaps the most important advantage of using a presentation is that the person making it can be flexible and can place his emphasis and arguments in accordance with the temperature of the meeting. I am not suggesting the case for being so flexible as to not put forward any solution. I am suggesting that, if the meeting is cold towards the recommendations, then the presenter has to spend more time on breaking down the resistance of the audience by establishing in more depth the advantages of what he is presenting. After all the work done during the pathfinding and designing stages, the individual concerned should have developed all the arguments, all the reasoning, and know all the answers to anything which may come from the audience.

It is essential for this selling process to be a confirmation of agreement which has already been reached with management. It should, in effect, be confirmatory selling which formalizes the individual detailed stages which the investigator has already agreed with management. To approach the audience completely cold, without any previous discussion, argument, and/or agreement, requires a great deal of ability and is almost certainly doomed to failure from the start. No management will readily agree to major proposals on the first hearing. Time is required to consider the effect of suggestions on departments, staff and on themselves, on the work they do, on their status and on many other important personal and individual points. To ask them to do this in the space of one meeting or one discussion is asking too much. The experienced man knows this and is able to handle it and obtain agreement from management in advance with little if any major resistance. It is not always possible to avoid awkward situations and dogmatic resistance from management during a presentation. The systems designer will have to face these problems. and be prepared for them, and be able to deal with them using his entire reserves of tact and patience.

Those wanting to go further into the art of presentation should read Anthony Jay's book *Effective presentation*.

Form design

Earlier in this chapter, when dealing with how the systems designer establishes what work should be done, the design of forms was mentioned. It is not intended to cover this subject in depth here, since there are several books available which deal solely with this subject. Perhaps the best of these is *Design of Forms in Government Departments* which is available from HMSO. In this section, the importance of good form design will be stressed and the main areas to be considered when designing forms will be indicated.

The form is a purely functional product. In exists to achieve a given purpose and must do this with the minimum of fuss. The aesthetic aspect of documents should be confined to portraying the company image and should be achieved without affecting the functional role of the document. A well-designed form is like a well-designed kitchen. It is carefully planned to reduce effort and drudgery to the minimum, and so that everything is to hand when required, and that anything not required can be disregarded. The benefits of a well-designed form become apparent only when the problems arising from poorly designed forms can be established. A well-designed form does its job with no fanfares, the poorly designed form will be mishandled and misused throughout the organization.

Examples of poorly designed forms and the benefits achieved when redesigned are manifest. To indicate the extent of the damaging effects of poorly designed forms a typical example is given below.

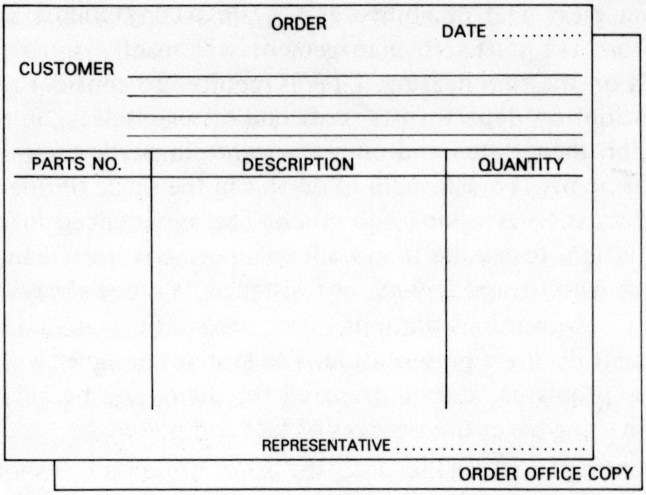

ORDER		DATE ....
CUSTOMER _____		

PARTS NO.	DESCRIPTION	QUANTITY

REPRESENTATIVE ....

ORDER OFFICE COPY

Fig. 6.1

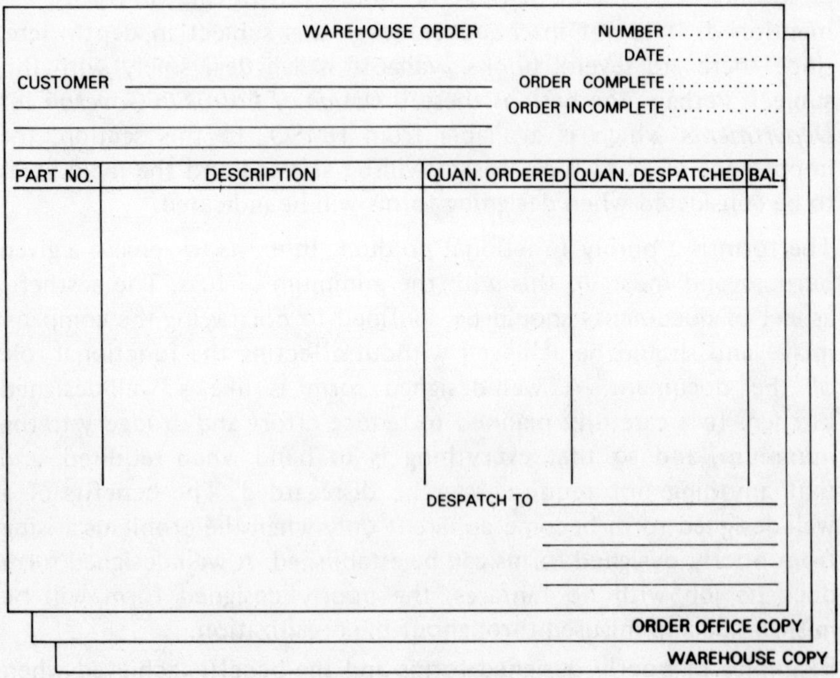

	WAREHOUSE ORDER	NUMBER...............
		DATE...............
CUSTOMER _____		ORDER COMPLETE ....
		ORDER INCOMPLETE ....

PART NO.	DESCRIPTION	QUAN. ORDERED	QUAN. DESPATCHED	BAL.

DESPATCH TO _____

ORDER OFFICE COPY

WAREHOUSE COPY

Fig. 6.2

The company concerned manufactured auto components. These were sold by representatives who collected orders from garages and by orders received direct from wholesalers or distributors (see Fig. 6.1). On receipt of the order, whether verbal or written, the order department prepared a warehouse order form (Fig. 6.2) which contained details of the parts required, the address where they should be sent and any special instructions.

The warehouse order form was sent to the warehouse where it was used to select the items from stock. A despatch note (Fig. 6.3) was prepared which detailed those items to be despatched, which might be only part of the total order.

A copy with the date of despatch was sent to the order office where the details were checked with the original warehouse order form. If there were any discrepancies a new outstanding warehouse order form was prepared and sent back to the warehouse. The despatch note was then priced and sent to the invoice clerk who prepared an invoice.

The forms which were to be examined and redesigned were the original order form, the warehouse order form and the despatch note. All these were completely different. If each form was considered separately, then it was not apparent that there was any missing information. However, if the procedure and

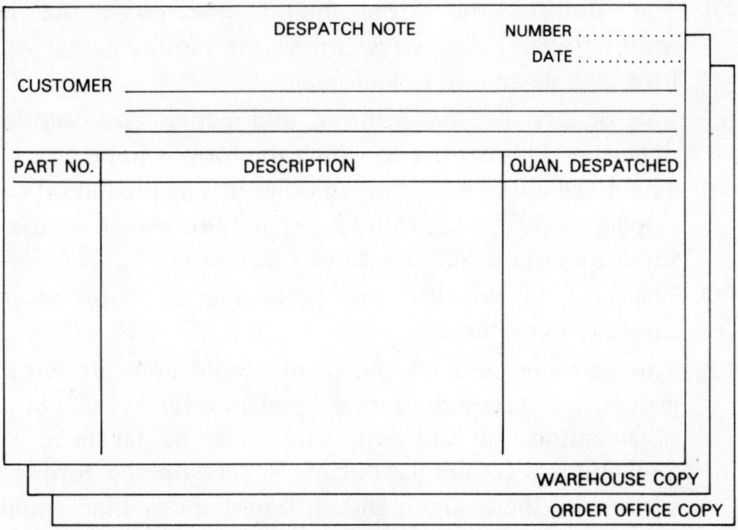

DESPATCH NOTE		NUMBER . . . .
		DATE . . . .
CUSTOMER		

PART NO.	DESCRIPTION	QUAN. DESPATCHED

WAREHOUSE COPY
ORDER OFFICE COPY

Fig. 6.3

purpose of the form were examined more fully, then the difficulty created by poor form design became apparent. The answer lay in redesigning one form to take the place of the three and good form design achieved this. When designing the solution to the problem, it became obvious that the invoice could also be incorporated as a copy of the new order form. The proper identification of a form's purpose is the key to good form design. Understanding the activities which take place at each stage of the processing of the form is a key to that design. This example shows that if activities are considered together, the purpose of the form is to notify the warehouse of parts ordered and for the warehouse to notify the customer of the items sent and for the customer to be invoiced. All these requirements are now achieved by the use of the new order set (see Fig. 6.4).

The following points should be considered by the form designer:

1. The form should be easy to read and easy to use
2. All activities and cross-referencing of information should be clearly noted on the form. Different colours or sections of the form could be used by different departments
3. The appearance of the form should fit in with generally accepted practices in the organization
4. The size of the form should meet with the basic international paper sizes unless the requirements for the form dictate an odd size of paper
5. The quality of the printing and paper used should be determined by the use to which the form is to be put
6. The make-up of the form, whether it is padded in sets, gum tipped, stapled, etc., should depend entirely on its use and the manner in which it is to be filed
7. The cost of printing and producing the form must be carefully considered
8. The wording used on the form should coincide with the generally accepted terms consistently used in the organization. In addition, care must be taken to avoid ambiguity, e.g., simply putting a date on the form is not sufficient, there are many different dates that could be applied, i.e., date of preparation, date of creation, or date of filing, etc.

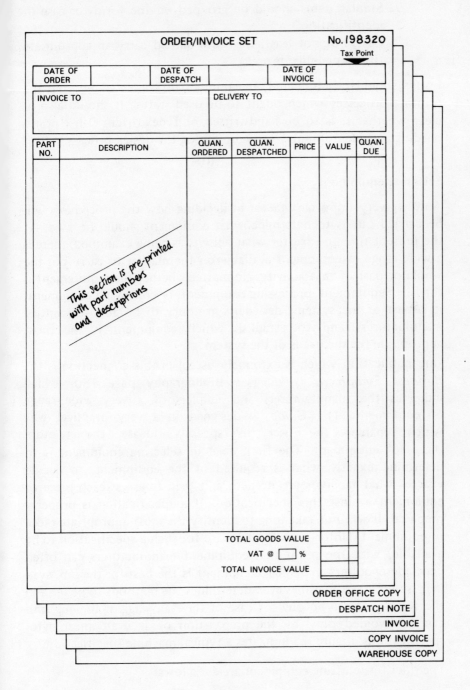

ORDER/INVOICE SET

No. 198320

Tax Point

DATE OF ORDER		DATE OF DESPATCH		DATE OF INVOICE	

INVOICE TO

DELIVERY TO

PART NO.	DESCRIPTION	QUAN. ORDERED	QUAN. DESPATCHED	PRICE	VALUE	QUAN. DUE

This section is pre-printed with part numbers and descriptions

TOTAL GOODS VALUE

VAT @ ☐ %

TOTAL INVOICE VALUE

ORDER OFFICE COPY

DESPATCH NOTE

INVOICE

COPY INVOICE

WAREHOUSE COPY

Fig. 6.4

9. Similar items should be grouped on the form for ease of identification

10. Last, but not least, the form should carry an appropriate title explaining its use.

Forms should be numbered, the number of copies stated, and the printing processes which ought to be used stated. It should also be clear whether it is to be handwritten or typewritten. Other points needing consideration may come up during the design process.

Selecting equipment

Another very important factor in deciding how the procedures will be carried out is to determine what equipment should be used. At the present time, no matter what activity is being examined, there is a wide range of equipment available on the market to carry out the whole or part of that activity. No matter whether the requirement is for filing equipment, processing equipment, or conveying equipment, it is part of the systems designer's armoury to be able to identify manufacturers and to establish which equipment is the most appropriate for the needs of the system.

One publication which is extremely useful in this connection is the *Business Equipment Guide* (see Bibliography page 180) which indicates the manufacturers and retailers of a very wide range of equipment. The *Guide* is designed in a very practical way which enables the user to speedily locate the relevant pieces of equipment. The first stage in selecting equipment is to determine exactly what is required of the equipment, to decide exactly what facilities are needed, and then to assess each piece of equipment against this specification. If a specification is properly prepared, it will not take long to identify the most appropriate piece of equipment. Unfortunately, it is rare for such a specification to be available, with the result that equipment manufacturers can often persuade enquirers that their equipment is the best for the job, even if it isn't. This sometimes even determines the methods to be used in the system. This is an obvious case of the 'tail wagging the dog' and can be avoided only by the preparation of accurate meaningful specifications. Figure 6.5 indicates a typical machine specification.

The rules for selecting equipment are as follows:

1. Clearly specify the requirements (see Fig. 6.5)

2. Consider the alternatives available and check each one against the following:
   (a) facilities required;
   (b) staffing required;
   (c) maintenance requirements;
   (d) cost—initial purchase cost and running cost.

EQUIPMENT REF.		MANUFACTURER		
		REQUIREMENTS		HOW MET
ACTIVITY	Sales invoicing			
WORK CONTENT	Input of standard product data			
	Input of customer data			
	Input of variable data			
	Preparation of invoice with extensions and VAT calculation			
	Code verification			
	Batch balancing			
	Output of data suitable for computer analysis			
WORK LOAD	Products 1000			
	Customers 550			
	Invoices per day 170			
	Lines per invoice 8			
COSTS	Initial purchase below £2500			
	Annual running cost below £2000			
	Stationery costs below £1000			
GENERAL REQUIREMENTS	Capable of on-line transmission of data to a computer			
	Minimum of operating skill			
	12 hours maintenance and repairs			
	No special environment			
	Capable of being programmed in-house			
	Continuing training facilities			

Fig. 6.5   Equipment specification

89

3. View short-listed equipment in actual operating circumstances. This can usually be arranged by the manufacturers and if it cannot then one should suspect the capability of that equipment
4. Obtain the opinion of other users of the equipment, either when viewing the equipment in operations or subsequently by correspondence or telephone
5. Ask for a demonstration of the equipment in the firm's premises where the equipment and the operation of it can be more closely related to its subsequent use. Some manufacturers will even programme their equipment as near to the final system as is feasible and demonstrate its suitability in this way
6. Decide finally on whether the performance of the equipment will meet requirements of the specification in all aspects. If it would appear to be weak in certain areas, ensure that the weaknesses are in the least important areas and that its strengths lie where major requirements demand.

The systems designer should not attempt to select equipment by himself. Knowledge and expertise in actual operating is extremely important, and for this the systems designer should consult the management and involve them in selecting the right equipment. There can often be situations where the choice between one or more pieces of equipment lies purely on the basis of personal preference, but where one piece of equipment has no clear advantage over another, it is better for management to make the selection. In addition, it is often useful to obtain the views of the staff who will be selected to operate the equipment. Brochures together with details of the equipment selected can add an additional emphasis to the recommendations in the systems designer's report. He should make use of the fact that this selection has been made by the managers concerned.

The new system

Having gone through the stages outlined in this chapter the systems designer now has the agreed new system in detailed form. The equipment required will have been selected, the forms will have been designed and the agreed procedures will have been examined. The new system is now complete. There remains only one job to do and that is to introduce it. Up to the present, the work of examining existing procedures, finding the existing paths, finding a new path, developing alternatives, designing the new system have all been carried out by an experienced individual who is independent of the operating management.

The introduction of a new system must now become the responsibility of the operating management. The systems designer can be available at all times to offer help and advice in the processes of introduction, but under no circumstances must he be responsible for this stage of the process. There is no way in which management can avoid their responsibility. They have accepted the recommendations and agreed to all the details of methods, machines, locations, etc. It is their full responsibility to introduce the new procedure effectively.

7 Introducing change

This subject is perhaps the most critical in successful control of paperwork. Change from both internal and external sources is inevitable. It is not simply acceptance of this fact which is vital, it is also the way in which change is handled.

In chapter 4 the poem 'The Calf Path' was quoted to illustrate man's desire for an easy life and how this is achieved by following in other people's footsteps. The problems of change must be fully considered by management and they must accept full responsibility for introducing change. The systems designer can offer help and advice, but on no account should he be called on to go beyond this.

Handling the introduction of change cannot be solved by following precise rules and checklists. It depends on the people concerned, their age, experience and temperament. A successful programme in one situation will fail totally in another. All that can be done is to be aware of the different problems associated with change and to follow a programme devised for each situation by careful analysis of the circumstances.

The steps involved in this analysis are:

Establish the changes created by new systems
Determine the human problems associated with these changes
Consider how to overcome these problems.

Establish the changes created by new systems

There are two different types of changes in the systems field. These can be described as:

Reactive change
Initiated change.

Reactive change

Reactive change occurs when events are allowed to overtake the activities concerned, and changes must be made to deal with these events. Such changes are often hurried and temporary; they rarely seem to cater fully with new circumstances. It is these which give rise to major problems in human terms.

Changes of a reactive nature are normally caused by such events as:

Take overs
Unplanned moves in business
Introduction of computers
Changes in senior management
System failures.

It is this kind of change which gives rise to the 'trouble-shooting' or 'fire-fighting' assignments which face many systems designers, and which are by far the worst type of assignment. This is because the people concerned are aware of the difficulties which exist, but are constantly seeking excuses and attempting to explain these difficulties rather than looking for solutions.

Any recommendations of the systems designer are an implied criticism of the existing situation which is often strongly defended. This human reaction gives rise to the problem of individuals taking intractable stands from which they find it difficult to move, without loss of face.

In a medium-sized engineering company, a particularly bad example of reactive change almost caused the business to close. The event was an unexpected demand for a newly developed product. The order/invoice department could not cope with the increase in volume and, though additional staff were employed, the overload of work increased. The staff became disillusioned, and irritated by the constant pressure of work. Turnover of staff was very high, and invoicing was two months behind. This so affected the cash flow that it became critical.

Changes were made in the staff and the system, but the constant backlog of work continued to frustrate attempts to improve the situation. Eventually a new office manager solved the problem by introducing a new system and subdividing the staff into two groups, one to deal with the backlog and the other to deal with the current situation. The longest serving group was given the job of dealing with backlogs, and the new staff of dealing with the current situation.

Reactive changes involve the following:

A backlog of work
Inadequate records

Unhappy staff
No time for adequate training
High staff turnover.

Initiated change

This kind of change is totally different and is much easier to deal with. The very nature of initiated changes, i.e., changes developed to improve existing systems which are already reasonably effective or to meet future needs, is such that careful planning and control of the changes avoids many of the associated problems.

Perhaps the reason for this stems from the need for the systems designer to involve all staff in the development of the new systems. For any new system to be successfully introduced it is essential to develop:

Enthusiam
Cooperation
Interest, and last but not least
Complete involvement in the Project.

In a project with which I was concerned the circular shown in Fig. 7.1 was sent to all those on the project team.

This kind of action, which is possible with initiated change, has a distinct advantage since it avoids the problems associated with reactive change.

Types of changes

When new systems are introduced, they may involve some of the following effects on the normal working routine of the staff concerned:

New procedures for carrying out activities
New activities to carry out
New forms
New machines and equipment
New offices
New locations
New people
New responsibilities.

DATE	4.3.75	FROM	T. J. Bentley		NUMBER	22

ITEM	DETAILS	TO BE NOTED	TO BE DISCUSSED	ACTION TO BE TAKEN BY
1.	**The effects of introducing change**			
	The effects of introducing change are not known in advance. The problem is to be able to predict and control any human problems which may arise. The ability to do this successfully will have a major effect on the implementation of the new system.	✓		
2.	We must expect a certain amount of resistance. Those concerned with the changes will try to assess the effect the changes will have on themselves personally. This will vary between individuals concerned.	✓		
3.	In implementing changes we cannot expect to do this perfectly and mistakes must arise. It is vital that these mistakes are noted in order to take corrective action, and to assess the success of such action.			✓ Systems Representative
4.	I suggest that a confidential record is maintained by the divisional/regional representative for each employee in the office, noting reactions and comments from the moment the staff are first notified of the changes, and subsequently after each training session.			✓ Systems Representative
5.	This record should contain details of employees, age, sex, and length of service and a section in which the details of courses attended, dates and reactions can be recorded.	✓		
6.	An alternative to the maintenance of a local record would be a survey covering the group and carried out on the basis of study groups organised as follows: 6.1 Group 1 detailed investigation in the normal office location. 6.2 Group 2 observed and interviewed during training. 6.3 Group 3 monitored indirectly as suggested in para. 4.		✓	
7.	The results of the above survey should contribute directly to the success of the implementation programme and point the way to introducing new changes wherever necessary. TJB/SEB/O&M/4.3.75	✓		

Fig. 7.1   Information circular

95

Each of these changes effects different people differently. While some may be easy to introduce in one situation, they will be almost impossible in another.

Every successful system is based on successful implementation and support of the staff at all levels. This is not possible without a full understanding of the human problems associated with the above changes.

Determining the human problems associated with change

When statements are made about people they are usually broad generalizations. Such statements may nevertheless have a basis of truth, but it must be emphasized that every person is different. Any general comment made about a person can only be used as a guide to his or her nature and behaviour.

In attempting to predict the effects of change it should be noted that there are three main categories of effects:

Physical effects
Psychological effects
Social effects.

PHYSICAL EFFECTS

When people are faced with physical changes in routine their first reaction is to examine these changes and to make their own assessment of the necessity. This means that such changes take some time to become effective and this kind of resistance should be accepted and understood.

Physical changes are perhaps the easiest to overcome. The following examples serve to indicate how important it is to be aware of and ready for resistance.

The office staff in a small office, who had for many years worked in the adjacent rooms, were faced with a change when the dividing wall was removed. Such a small step even produced a question of who was to be made redundant. To the local management such a small change was thought to be unimportant.

In a large office it was decided to change the method of handling outgoing mail. The existing system involved a collection at 4.00 p.m. This was considered too early by many managers and a new system was introduced whereby mail was delivered to the mail room by the secretaries at any time up to 5.00 p.m. The immediate effect was that two secretaries resigned because they regarded delivering mail as beneath them.

PSYCHOLOGICAL EFFECTS

When any change is in the offing each individual asks himself, 'How does this affect me?' Too often an unaware or naive management attempt to introduce changes without recognizing that this basic question will arise.

The individual goes further than simply to ask this question. He endeavours to produce his own answers, and in so doing may make inaccurate assumptions. One or two individuals may take it upon themselves to explain these changes to their colleagues, and so understandably concern grows and spreads.

Perhaps the most important questions in a person's mind are:

'Can I cope with this?'
'Am I too old or too young?'
'Will I be able to work fast enough?'

Nothing concerns a person more than whether or not he can carry out his work in a competent manner. Changes can threaten his confidence. This may create resistance.

SOCIAL EFFECTS

Social effects are those which are connected with a person's relationships with others. The framework of these relationships is often established by the technology and organization of the work added to the physical environment.

These internal, social relationships are extremely important to the individual, who will be concerned to see how he may be affected by change.

A manager of an Area Office was promoted to manage the Regional Office in a city. Perhaps it is predictable that several questions will be raised in his mind.

'Will my wife settle down in the suburbs?'
'Can I get on with a large staff?'
'What will the car allowance be?'
'That assistant manager—he was my rival for the job—will he cooperate with me?'
'Will I have an office carpet?'
'Is it all worth it?'

Of course, the effects of change are influenced by individual and collective attitudes towards change. The general factors which determine these attitudes may be categorized as follows:

Innate attitudes to change
Insecurity
The rules (norms) of a society
Trust
Past events.

1. Innate attitudes to change

From childhood to maturity the individual has to be disciplined in order to function within society. This progressive disciplining may be accomplished by offering suitable rewards. The result may be that there is relatively little innate resistance to change, but on the other hand, forcing a person to yield to what he considers are unreasonable demands may result in a residue of suspicion and fear.

2. Insecurity

The need for security is built into an individual's personality and upbringing, i.e., the environment in which he has lived. The need for security affects behaviour. In general, the secure individual is self-confident; and he is normally resourceful and flexible in his attitudes.

It is essential that management wishing to implement change should realize that resistance to that change will manifest itself in suspicion, and, occasionally, distrust.

3. The rules (norms) of a society

As we have already seen, the sociologist suggests that the individual operates in several different spheres, each with his own culture, e.g., the work group, the darts team, the town community, and so on. The work group will establish its accepted norms to which its members are expected to conform. These norms may be formal, i.e., those developed by the group itself within the framework of the formal or legally accepted norms. As an example, although the formal rules may prescribe a 15-minute mid-morning break commencing at 10.00 a.m., the group—and the management—may tacitly accept that the break be taken at a convenient time during the work process and may last up to 25 minutes.

In any business organization, the norms of society are often accepted implicitly and are rarely questioned. This perpetuates existing practices. Challenging existing practices in industry can have interesting results, as an examination of some current practices reveals:

Long service with a firm is desirable
Overtime is essential and unavoidable
Fringe benefits should be in proportion to the status of the job
Skilled workers must only function within the limits of their skills.

4. Trust

Interaction between individuals and groups over a period of time will establish the patterns of mutual trust or otherwise. In the work situation, trust may be developed between the single employee, his supervisor, his union representative and the management. Where trust has not been developed, change may be implemented slowly if explicit, written guarantees are given by management. However, it is obvious that such an environment of distrust can rarely foster successful results.

5. Past events

The previous history within the firm clearly influences attitudes towards change. People, understandably, often regard past events as precedents for what is likely to occur in the future. Such past events may be either external to the firm or internal.

External factors
  (a) Unemployment in the region
  (b) Alternative sources of employment
  (c) Mobility of labour.
Internal factors
  (a) The firm's past policy practice and custom
  (b) Style of management
  (c) The manner in which the previous changes have been accomplished.

These attitudes will be reflected in the questions the individual asks his supervisor.

Questions relating to the individual and his work
Questions related to the individual and his colleagues
Questions related to the individual and the organization.

Individual reactions to change

The individual or the group can behave within two extremes when faced with change—deliberate sabotage or enthusiastic cooperation; this is shown diagramatically in Fig. 7.2.

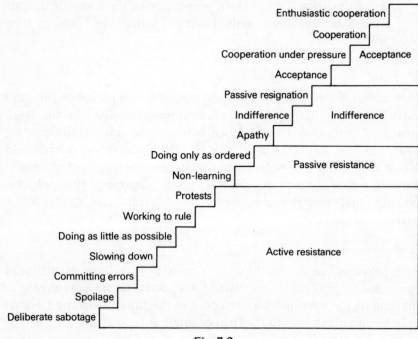

Fig. 7.2

Predicting the pattern of behaviour will depend on the knowledge of the situation and of the individuals and groups involved. It may be possible to draw up a kind of balance sheet of assumed losses and gains. However, it should be stressed that valuable as such analysis may be, it remains incomplete. It is not possible to anticipate every question and reaction. Nonetheless, such an exercise does enable the manager to marshal his argument in the most persuasive manner possible. He can then identify those particular areas of resistance where persuasion may fail so that alternative means of solving the problem of change can be considered.

Overcoming the human problems of change

It should be accepted that universal cooperation will rarely be achieved, even in the most favourable circumstances. Some resistance—or inertia—will be met with. Having considered these areas of possible resistance, what methods are available to the manager to overcome resistant behaviour?

Compulsion

The employment of statutory authority (compulsion) as a means of bringing about the change will almost certainly increase pressures on staff under compulsion thereby causing frustration and aggression. Threats and bribes—the essential tools of compulsion—are unwise and undesirable, increasing resistance rather than reducing it.

Persuasion

Persuasion demands the ability to look at the situation from another's viewpoint; in particular, the other person's needs and goals. Persuasion depends on the presentation of a balance between possible losses and the promise of rewards. Such rewards must be relevant to and must outweigh the reasons for resistance. The rewards may be economic—direct or in fringe benefits; perhaps by the increase in status, by changing the pattern of interrelationships, etc.

Redundancy

Change often brings fear of redundancy in its wake. Fulfilling a pledge of 'no redundancy' may be extremely difficult, but should be considered, in many cases, as a desirable objective. A less desirable alternative may be the promise to maintain incomes for those who are 'surplus to requirements'. In all cases, detailed consideration of an individual's natural desire for security should be understood.

Communication

In general, the more widespread the understanding of all aspects of change, the less likely there will be resistance. The following questions should be answered.

> What are the short-term and long-term objectives to be accomplished by the change?
> Why need these objectives be accomplished?
> What is to be changed—and how?
> When will the change occur?
> Who will be involved and how will they be affected?
> What will be the situation after the change?
> What are the potential benefits that might be gained from the change?

Management can transmit information by written or spoken word. Such information should be accessible, factual and accurate. It should be presented in an acceptable form and should answer the questions. Finally, it should be clear to both management and employees that understanding has been achieved. Face to face discussion, either with individuals or with a group, is by far the best way of developing a two-way interchange, whether meetings are formal or otherwise. Face to face discussion ensures that answers are given to questions of genuine concern to the people involved.

Timing
In general, the longer the time between announcement of pending change and its initiation, the lower the resistance. Conversely, the greater the resistance the longer it takes to realize the change.

Participation
As a general rule, the extent of personal involvement in making decisions about change, the less will be the resistance. However, participation is not something which can be established overnight. The environment should be developed in which people want to participate and such an environment will be nourished by the quality of the feelings and attitudes of the people involved, particularly with respect to their mutual trust. Management seeking participation should also feel secure and not regard discussion periods as a sign of weakness. Clearly, also, management should enter discussion with an open mind to the possibility of alternative approaches and should recognize openly contributions made by the staff.

Planning to make change
Management should, when dealing with change, attempt to specify the exact nature of the change at the outset, anticipate the effects on the people involved, examine the possible solutions to anticipated problems, and develop a timetable for action. The following questions may be put:
1. What are the objectives of the change, both in short- and long-range terms? To what extent are these goals desirable? To what extent are they possible?
2. What is the proposed method for accomplishing the change? How is it introduced and implemented? How strong is the commitment to one particular method? Can other methods be used provided that the objectives are achieved?

3. What is the justification for making the proposed change? What are the expected benefits? Who will gain?
4. Who originated the idea for change? What is his motivation for proposing the change? How much support is there for the change?
5. By what date must the change be achieved? Would it be possible first to test the change experimentally with a trial group?
6. Who will be directly affected? Who will be involved in the introduction and implementation of the change?
7. Who is responsible and accountable for realizing the expected benefits from the change? What are the sources of assistance the manager can employ in accomplishing the change?

Having disciplined his approach to the problem, the manager may then anticipate the effects on those involved. Finally, he should attempt to draw up a timetable in which the separate elements whether independent or interdependent in the progression of the change are considered. The logic of the interdependent elements will determine the order in which the tasks should be accomplished.

Conclusion

Change is inevitable in a business that is to prosper in a changing environment. To accomplish change is a complicated and difficult process.

Change affects people in many ways. Our attitudes to it are governed by many factors. Management should attempt to understand what these are and then, in some measure, be able to anticipate the reaction of individuals and groups. Anticipation will allow management to adopt a satisfactory method of minimizing resistance.

Part 3
Controlling paperworkers

8 The right environment

So far, our main consideration has been the systems used by the paperworker and the ways in which efficient systems can be designed. In addition we have discussed the importance of the staff's involvement in the design of these systems and human problems involved in change. In this chapter, the tools available to the paperworker will be examined. Tools, in this context, cover a very wide field including the office itself, the way in which the office is laid out, the equipment, the working methods, the volume of work, the quality required, communication facilities and computers.

Office design and conditions

The way in which an office is laid out can determine the efficiency with which work is done. Layout, here, means the planning of related activities, so that the amount of movement and the amount of disturbance caused in the transfer of paperwork from one job to the next is minimized. Correct layout of offices is not achieved in a haphazard way. It is achieved by careful consideration of the work to be done in that office, of the needs of the staff and of the best way in which those needs can be met. There are many office equipment and furniture manufacturers who will provide a planning service in order to ensure efficient layout. This is a very useful service, but it presupposes that the management is aware of its requirements and is able to give the planners some guidance.

Perhaps the best way of showing the importance of layout would be to give some guidelines and to incorporate these guidelines in the example of office layout covered in detail in Appendix 4.

The main principles to be considered when examining the layout of an office are as follows:

1. Define the purpose of the office
2. Establish the limiting factors, i.e., height, floor space, room structure, etc.

3. Determine the occupants of the office
4. Consider the status limits if these exist
5. Examine the equipment which has to be housed in the office
6. Carefully consider the services required, i.e., heating, lighting, telephones, etc.
7. The requirements of the Offices, Shops and Railways Premises Act, 1963
8. The relationships of departments
9. Security, i.e., information, fire and theft
10. The amount of movement in the office, and the movement in and out of the office
11. Levels of noise.

When the above factors have been considered it is necessary to decide upon the positioning of desks and equipment within the overall area of the office. This can be tackled in three main ways.

1. The individual office
2. The open office
3. The landscaped office.

All three methods of office layout are used in British offices, but there is a preference at present for the landscaped office. This last is, however, much more difficult to establish because it involves considerable expense, in terms of acoustic requirements, carpets, tiles, etc. It is not intended to deal with the benefits or disadvantages of each of these three methods here. The following sections will, however, set down the principles involved in achieving efficient layout and also provide guidelines for the approach, when planning a new office or a revision of existing layouts.

Principles and approach to successful office layout
The main principles are as follows:
1. Ensure that the floor space is sufficient for the needs of the occupants. Note that the Offices Act requires a minimum of 400 cubic feet per person (approx. 11.2 m^3)
2. That the flow of work in the office is such as to minimize movement between desks and also between movement in and out of the office itself
3. Office equipment should be located very carefully ensuring a minimum of distraction to other occupants

4. Lighting should be carefully considered so that each paper-worker has sufficient light, and that this comes from above, and not immediately behind, which would cast a shadow on the desk
5. Decorations in the office should be restful to the eyes and not too bright.

When considering the layout of an office, the result is likely to be successful if the next steps are followed.

1. Prepare a scale plan
2. Cut out scale shapes for each piece of equipment and desk
3. Lay these on the plan and find what appears to be the best solution, bearing in mind the previous factors
4. When a possible solution has been established draw round the shapes and have a look at the final plan
5. When this is agreed mark the positions for electrical sockets and telephones, bearing in mind the purpose of each job
6. Ensure that the relationship of size and space allows the office to appear well balanced and not to be too cramped or too widespread.

It is as well at this point to remind you that a desk is itself a work place and must cater for the following.

1. Incoming work
2. Work in progress
3. Outgoing work
4. Storage of equipment and immediate files
5. Calculators, typewriters, etc.

The careful design of a person's working unit is absolutely essential for effective operation. Reference to Appendix 4 will show how careful planning can provide an environment for efficient paperwork. The Offices, Shops and Railway Premises Act, 1963, sets out the facilities to be provided for the paperworker. Its provisions cover cleanliness, overcrowding, temperature, ventilation, lighting, sanitary conveniences, general welfare requirements, training, operation of machines, fire precautions and duties of employers and employees. It is not intended to set down these details in this book as the abstract of the act which is available from the HMSO does so in very readable form.

Assessing work content

Perhaps the most important factor in equipping the paperworker correctly is to know fully what his job involves, and to know exactly what equipment is required to enable that job to be done efficiently. This is far more than the usual concept of work measurement. In assessing work content we are not just concerned with the volume of work to be done, but with the nature of that work, and to assess the right tools for the job. Assessing work content is a detailed and lengthy procedure in many cases and requires a form of analysis which for the sake of simplicity is set out in full detail in Appendix 5. The principles of assessing work content are indicated below. These principles have been applied in the format provided in Appendix 5 and in many practical cases where this format has been followed, a successful conclusion has been reached, i.e., the paperworker has had the right equipment, the right kind of desks and files, with which to carry out his job.

Principles of assessing work content

1. A detailed analysis of the job to be done indicating the forms to be used and the sequence of operation
2. Details of the amount of work to be done
3. A breakdown of the job into different aspects as indicated in Appendix 5, i.e., filing, sorting, processing, collating, etc.
4. A measure of the level of work, i.e., routine, discretionary, initiative, etc.
5. The relationships between this job and other jobs demanding a knowledge of paperwork flow requirements
6. An understanding of the communication requirements of the job
7. Details of the timing of work and of the accuracy requirements
8. The relationship of this job to others in terms of the timing and frequency of the systems within which the particular activity fits.

These principles of assessing work content can be explained and discussed in more detail when a particular job is examined. This form of example is given in Appendix 5, and by working through this the reader will develop an understanding of the needs for careful and controlled assessment of work content.

Equipment requirements

A paperworker's equipment requirements are assessed by reference to the work content. From this can be established precisely the kind of equipment needed. This could vary across the whole range, and it is part of the system designer's function to know the full range of equipment available. He needs to know about the many office machines available: calculators, typewriters, dictating machines, etc., or even about computer terminals. On the other hand, all that may be needed could be a pad and a pencil.

Buying equipment will not be dealt with in this book, but suffice it to say that a careful analysis of the needs of the job will lead to the selection of the piece of equipment which primarily meets those needs at a realistic cost.

One current example of a problem in choosing business machines is the small pocket or desk calculator. There are a large number available at varying prices, all with very similar characteristics, and it is only when one comes to examine reliability, servicing and cost of maintenance, that the best one can be found.

Workflow

Workflow is perhaps one of the least considered factors within most offices. This is of primary importance to the successful working of any system and can be best illustrated by an example with which I recently had to deal.

In a regional sales office of a large company, they were using or planning to use computer terminals. Changing the flow of work from one of preparing batches of documentation for invoicing on a computer, to actually inputting those batches through the terminal caused many problems. The main problem was the belief of the local staff that one fully trained operator could input all the data produced by four clerks. This, of course, gave rise to its own problem, how to ensure a flow of work from the four clerks to the operator, in order to balance the workload across the whole day. What frequently occurred was that the clerks finished their work towards the end of the day, and left a late peak workload for the operator. This was both frustrating and annoying for the operator who spent several sessions during the morning with nothing to do and often had to work overtime in order to complete the day's work. Obviously this was not a satisfactory state of affairs. It was only alleviated when it was decided that each clerk should become a terminal operator, and input her own work when completed, thus ensuring a balanced flow of work. At certain times, of course, this solution did mean that one or more girls were ready to use the terminal at the same time, but this was overcome by the girl continuing with her other duties until such time as the terminal was free.

The above example is one simple but important example of how lack of thought given to the flow of work in an office can create chaos; another example is when the flow of work does not provide the information when it is needed to start the next function along the line.

An example of this type of problem is the relationship between the order office and the despatch point. The order office received the orders during the afternoon and sent the details through to the despatch point by phone. The following morning a typed confirmation sheet of the orders was sent to the despatch point. However, by this time many loads had been despatched and often the confirmation sheet showed that errors had been recorded during the previous afternoon's telephone conversation. The solution to this problem was to use tele-copiers by which the order sheets prepared in the order office were sent across the telephone line and received at the despatch point in the evening of the day on which the orders were taken. This sheet represented the confirmation sheet which had usually been sent the following morning. The effects were considerable. Very few errors were made and the information was available much quicker, resulting in a greater degree of customer satis-faction.

Within the office, workflow between departments is also of consider-able importance. One department's end results are probably the start point of the next department. It is important that this relationship is given the correct amount of consideration.

Cash was received by the cashiers, totalled and checked and paid into the bank by a certain time during the day, the next operation was the allocation of that cash to the sales ledger. This had to wait until the cash was banked. This, of course, meant that the cashier's office worked in the morning and the sales ledger allocation in the afternoon. This obviously was not satisfactory. The solution was the speeding up of the processes for each department by dividing the cheques and remittance advices, so that once the two had been balanced the recording of the cheques could take place while cash allocation was being done from the remittances. This might seem an elementary problem, but then most of the problems of workflow are elementary when analysed, but cause so much trouble when unrecognized.

Determining and solving workflow problems can be done following the assessing of work content and in the relationships of jobs. Flowcharts are invaluable in assessing workflow. It is one of the primary aims of the systems designer to ensure that efficient workflow is as much a part of his systems as correct documentation.

Quality control

Quality control in the office is of paramount importance as lack of it causes a considerable increase in paperwork. Not only does any error have to be corrected, but the effect of inaccurate information given to management and customer dissatisfaction can be far reaching. In some instances, it has almost caused the collapse of the business. Quality control in the office can be achieved by following a carefully thought out programme of checking and controlling work as it takes place. There are three principal forms of quality which are required in an office.

1. Accuracy
2. Legibility
3. Timing.

Accuracy

This is controlled by building into the system checking sequences, such as batch balancing. This establishes a total that must be achieved at the end of the batch. By using an adding machine or accounting machine to total the individual entries into the system the batch can be balanced. Modern equipment allows for a variety of accuracy checks and wherever possible these should be incorporated. Providing for accuracy can be done in three main ways:

1. Effective training
2. Checks which can be 100 per cent check sample or spot checks
3. Mechanization.

The types of errors made can be listed under the following headings.

Transcription
Calculation
Filing
Sorting
Coding.

Accuracy in all of these is essential to the efficient operation of any system. To overcome these problems requires careful thought and planning. In the case of transcription, the aim should be to eliminate the need for transcription wherever possible by using three in one systems, i.e., the design of paperwork which allows three entries to be made at one writing. These are currently used in many manual ledger applications and in accounting machine systems. It should also be possible to limit the numbers of characters which need to be transcribed by using key reference codes wherever possible. Calculation errors can be avoided by the use of machines and ready reckoners instead of the fallible human brain. Filing can be controlled if the documents to be filed are clearly marked and if staff have been effectively trained to file properly. Sorting requires a similar clear definition. Coding can be overcome by the use of simple codes, and properly prepared code lists. If the code can be related directly to the subject matter by the use of mnemonics and alphabetical characters, then coding should be easy and errors from this source virtually eliminated.

Legibility

This can be achieved by good training, the use of equipment, such as typewriters, accounting machines, and by effective printing and form design. If sufficient space and sufficient indication are given on forms as to the data to be entered, then there is no reason for illegibility and the problems it causes. In discussing training, it is absolutely essential to ensure that the paperworker whose job is not entirely dealing with paperwork, but who often is the source of prime data, fully understands the use to which information will be put in the system.

A recent example of how important this was occurred during an exercise of sales data input to a computer based system. It was established that of the four key codes to be entered into the computer, three were in fact entered on the documentation by the man delivering the goods, whose job was only partially that of paperwork.

When it was clearly pointed out to this man that three of the items entered into the computer were originated by his entries on the document he became much more concerned with the legibility and accuracy of the data he entered.

This example shows how training in avoiding errors must be carried throughout the systems and throughout the company; it must be extended to every point where data is originated and handled.

Timing

The ability to control the timing of work requires good work planning and careful scheduling. There are numerous examples which could be listed of where a lack of these qualities has caused considerable difficulty. However, there is no point in using examples of what is a straightforward, but often overlooked, practice. In nearly every instance when paperwork is done, there is a time limit which may or may not be recognized, but which nevertheless exists within the system. It is only by assessing the work and by determining the timing and its importance within each job, that the workflow can be ensured.

Errors usually occur in three main ways:

1. Worker fault
2. Management fault
3. Faulty methods.

The first of these can be overcome as indicated above by good training and provision of the right tools for the job, including equipment and form design. When this fails to correct the problem then quite naturally the ability of the paperworker concerned must be examined. If it is found that this job is too much for him, he should be given something easier to do rather than continually attempt to put right the errors.

Management fault often occurs in incorrect instruction, in misunderstandings of requirements and in general attitudes towards effectiveness of the staff. When supervision is lacking, and when staff are unaware of the difficulties caused by errors, they become lax and they are not entirely to blame for it. Management should clearly take the responsibility and put its house in order.

Faulty methods should be covered by the type of systems design discussed in previous chapters, and if this is done carefully in sufficient detail then faulty methods should not cause errors. In many cases of changing circumstances, new staff and a lack of effective systems control, faulty methods do cause a number of errors.

Communications in the office

It is not my purpose to discuss in depth the problems of communications and how these can be overcome, but simply to state that communications in the office are a vital function which must be catered for by careful analysis of needs and a careful choice of the correct equipment to meet those needs. This is an area where the system designer should concentrate. The vast range of communication equipment provides him with tremendous choice to meet these needs.

The underlying principles of successful communication should be to pass the required information to the person concerned, with a minimum of effort and with a maximum of understanding. This is rarely done by the use of the internal memo. It is rarely done by copious written reports. It is most successfully done face to face or by the use of telephones. In each situation the most appropriate means of communications should be used, e.g., well-designed forms. The point is that good communications should be considered a need within the paperwork systems being developed. They are vital, and should be catered for adequately. The problems of getting people to talk to each other will be dealt with in a subsequent chapter. Needless to say, without an effective communication system in a business, paperwork itself accumulates and is far less effective than if communications were successful. In deciding upon a communications system, it is necessary to know what must be communicated to whom. Only then can formal guidelines be established to ensure that successful communications take place.

In order to ensure effective communications, the problems within the business must be fully understood and throughout this book the aim has been to analyse and detail activities so that a greater understanding is available to all those concerned with system design, including the design of effective communications.

The computer and the paperworker

The computer should be considered by the systems designer as just another piece of equipment. Computers themselves are extremely useful in certain situations and have tremendous capacity for work of a routine and of an arithmetical nature. In the right situations there is no doubt that computers should be used, but in using them efficiently we are faced with considerable problems.

To the paperworker the computer means a need for greater accuracy and a need for an understanding of the processing requirements. Forms should be designed in such a way that data preparation is made easy and can be done quickly by punch operators, key to disc operators, or terminal operators.

The curse of their job is inaccurately prepared data for computer input. It is this emphasis upon accuracy and quality, including timing, which is a change from the normal manual system.

It is essential that controls are established which ensure that the results coming from the computer are matched to the totals of the data which are input. The ability to use large computer-based file systems should provide reduced needs for filing and storage in the office. This does not always occur because of:

1. The need for files for immediate answers in the local offices
2. The distrust of management and paperworkers for computer based files
3. The problems associated with programming in the system to allow access to files.

Classification and coding of data also becomes of paramount importance as a computer works almost entirely on numerical data, the accuracy of which is essential to obtaining good results. The principles of systems design outlined in previous chapters apply equally to systems using computers, and to those using any other equipment. The proper specification of the needs of the system and of the work content are all essential regardless of the equipment used.

Conclusion

In providing the paperworker with the right environment, the systems designer must be at pains to see that nothing in the environment detracts from carrying out the system. It is important that paperworkers enjoy their work within the system and do not feel in any way limited or constrained by their environment. Providing the right tools, for work to be done in the right way, at the right time, by the right people is essentially the task of the systems designer.

9 Setting the right example

It is very important for senior management to realize that most attitudes and practices of junior staff are the result of imitating supervisory staff. This simple statement is true, and there is no greater service a manager can give to a company than by setting the right example.

When a new recruit joins a company he watches other employees, particularly his supervisors, to establish the accepted standards of behaviour. Current practices in an office are often followed by new inhabitants with a zeal which is as misplaced as it is dangerous.

There is only one way to ensure staff follow sensible and well-developed methods of working and have the right attitudes towards work. That is by setting the right example.

Senior staff inevitably set examples and often these are based on the tenuous principle that seniority has its privileges. They often act according to the doctrine of 'Do as I say' not 'Do as I do'. This is not only harmful—it destroys trust and respect.

There are a great many areas in which the principle of setting the right example is beneficial. I have selected the following areas for further consideration. These are areas which, in my opinion, are the most important and most often encountered in offices.

Timekeeping
Filing
It must be typed
Quality
Do it now
Send me a report.

Timekeeping

Perhaps one of the most difficult areas of controlling paperworkers is the establishment and maintenance of timekeeping and punctuality.

It appears in most offices that the need for punctuality diminishes with seniority. This is frequently justified on the basis that seniority implies trustworthiness. Though this might be true, I maintain that it is difficult if not impossible to get staff to conform to precise times without supervisory staff doing the same.

If strict starting and finishing times are used, then everyone ought to keep to those times and work longer if necessary. However, in practice, the inflexibility of such a system works to the company's detriment.

In a company in which I worked, the computer department was managed by two successive managers. The first manager was a typical 9.00 till 5.00 man, and naturally his staff acted accordingly. From time to time when emergencies called for overtime, he found his staff unwilling and uncooperative. When the new manager took over, his attitude was different and both he and his staff worked within flexible time limits all being judged on successful performance of duties, not timekeeping. In this case overtime as such was never necessary though long hours were worked now and again.

Flexible working hours systems have been introduced in a variety of companies, and in certain government departments. The principle of flexible hours is the operation of a basic core of time with flexible periods of time at each end of the core.

In Fig. 9.1 the choice available to staff can be clearly seen. A simple recording system is used to accumulate the hours worked for each member of staff. At the end of a given period, i.e., weekly or monthly, the hours worked are compared with the basic

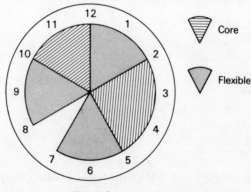

Fig. 9.1

120

requirement. The difference is either time owed to the company or time owed to the person. Certain proprietary systems are available with or without computer based recording systems.

Results of the flexible hours system vary, but are considered by most of the experimenting companies to have been successful. The principal benefits claimed are:

1. Greater motivation
2. Less absenteeism
3. Higher individual output
4. Better quality of work.

Whether or not a company should operate fixed or variable hours depends upon the circumstances, a careful analysis of the flow of work, and timing of activities. Whichever method is chosen management must ensure that attention is directed towards successful performance of duties, rather than simply working so many hours.

Filing

As I have stated previously, filing is a task which is given to the most inexperienced staff. They are shown how to file by their predecessors. Bad habits and incorrect methods of filing are thereby perpetuated. The most common practices are:

1. Filing in the wrong place
2. Filing unnecessary copies
3. Inconsistency, i.e., Sir Jonas Bloggs filed under S, J and B
4. Illogical filing.

Frequently managers can be heard to say that they would not know where to find anything if the person responsible for their filing left.

If managers and supervisors showed their staff how and what to file and set an example, then considerable volumes of paper could be dispensed with.

Some time ago I met a secretary who explained to me why she typed three or more copies of every letter, etc. One was filed alphabetically under the recipient, one was filed chronologically and one under the subject concerned. If copies were sent to anyone other than the recipient, then one copy was made out for each and filed accordingly. The girl's time was divided into 30 per cent typing and 70 per cent filing. The reason given by the boss was that he had all his correspondence filed in whatever form he might need it. Needless to say the boss couldn't be bothered to use a priority or cross-referencing system and eventually had to employ a filing clerk.

The danger when filing of setting bad examples or not even bothering, lies in the build-up of large volumes of unnecessary paper and in creating in new staff a complete misunderstanding of the principles of filing. Of course, the manager must himself understand filing principles to set a good example. Perhaps this is where the problem lies.

It must be typed

Typing is an accepted activity within the office. The scope and volume of typed work is vast. Typewriters have been one of the most well-developed and most used form of office machine. They have a variety of attachments and devices and vary in price from £50 to over £3000.

Typing is also an area which has been subjected to long study in order to see how the conversion from written or recorded data to typescript can be made more efficient. In most instances the answer is simple—'Don't type it'.

This simple answer is acceptable to most people except, it seems, to typists and their employers. This attitude towards typing has been created by the setting of a somewhat expensive and unnecessary example. To have something typed requires the services of a typist and this implies status. I would maintain that only certain work should be typed, perhaps covering—

    Reports
    Minutes
    External correspondence
    Legal documents
    Circulars and forms.

Each company can, of course, decide upon its own list of typed documents. All other documentation could be handwritten and other communication made verbally.

This aim of reducing typing must start somewhere if the increasing costs of this service are to be reduced. I would suggest that this start should be made by senior management, whose example would then be followed.

Quality

The quality and accuracy of many clerical jobs is crucial and any reduction of quality in these jobs would be expensive and time-consuming in error correction. There are, however, a great many other tasks in which this degree of quality is unnecessary.

It is again the task of management to sort out each type of work and to ensure all unnecessary checking routines are eliminated. Management must be made to appreciate the extent of the work involved when they ask for something to be accurate. Perhaps the cost should be calculated and management asked if they are prepared to pay for the relatively small increase in accuracy, which may have little value.

I recall an incident concerning a printing department which printed documents for internal use. One of these documents was the internal memo. The managing director had intimated that the quality wasn't very good. This was interpreted by his secretary as meaning the quality should be improved. This was done and the result was a trebling in the paper cost and a doubling in the printing cost. The total annual increase in cost was £1500. No one else in the company had commented. During a review of stationery costs the fact was pointed out to the managing director who denied he had ever asked for the quality to be increased. This was, of course, true, but his brief comment on quality was acted upon to the detriment of the company's profits.

Do it now

The timing of work is one of those aspects of paperwork which it is very difficult to establish. In different companies the timing of various work differs widely, and in fact there appears to be no consistent practice. The nearest one comes is the closing of purchase ledgers sometime in the first two weeks of the following month.

The responsibility for establishing efficient timing is management's and they should take this responsibility seriously. The cost of carrying out certain paperwork tasks, particularly the production of relevant operating statistics, can be very high in any case, but the amount of overtime pay or the cost of additional staff employed to meet unnecessarily tight schedules is enormous. Such pressure of work is a monthly occurrence in many accounting departments. Usually when one asks why the work is done in this way it is because the boss has requested it. Perhaps he should be asked whether he would rather have it the following day and save the extra cost, which is often very high in annual terms.

In a company with several operating divisions, each of the financial controllers prepared the accounts at different dates varying from the 15th to the 25th of the following month. All results had to be ready for the same board meeting. The reasons for the different dates varied, but there is no doubt that the cost of preparing the accounts was higher in the divisions who prepared them first. The reason for the variation in the timing was originally because of joint use of a central facility. The result was nothing more than a divisional race.

How can supervisors and managers expect junior staff to work efficiently and use common sense when they themselves are often guilty of doing neither.

Send me a report

No other request is more misused than 'Send me a report'. It is used to avoid immediate consideration of a problem. No doubt it is based on the principle that if it is ignored it will go away.

When a manager asks for a report he could mean one of the following:

'Send me a report.'
'Go away.'
'I'm not interested.'
'Don't send me a report.'
'Go and find something to do.'

It is not usually clear to the subordinate what his boss means, and even after seeking clarification he may interpret it as meaning quite literally 'Send me a report'.

This means that the report writer has to prepare a draft, have it typed, rewrite it, have it retyped then corrected. It can then be submitted.

The recipient must read it, make notes, reread it, then either reply or discuss it with his subordinate. Last but not least, a decision must be made to act upon or ignore the report's recommendations.

There are, of course, many occasions when a report is necessary. Report writing is an acquired skill, which many junior managers have not yet acquired. This may be a reason for asking them to write reports, but I doubt it. It is up to senior staff to decide when reports are necessary and for what purpose; beyond this communication of ideas and suggestions can be done quite successfully if only people will talk to each other. Face to face contact seems to be strenuously avoided, and is made more difficult by the construction of offices on the basis of tiers of rabbit hutches with everyone in his own little office. *Ad hoc* face to face discussions as and when required are perhaps the most effective means of communication available. Yet they are frequently replaced by memos and messages passed on second hand, lacking emphasis and delaying response.

The fact that all the practices denigrated above are still to be found flourishing in most offices is due entirely to the failure of supervisors and managers to set the right example.

10 Getting people to
   talk to each other

Throughout this book I have attempted to indicate the problems caused by the proliferation and lack of control of paperwork, and how the problems can be overcome. I have dealt in some detail with the methods of systems design which I have used successfully for many years.

I have found, however, by experience that the elimination of unnecessary paperwork is made much easier if people talk to each other. So, in this the final chapter, I am going to discuss the benefits of this method. In addition, I offer some thoughts and ideas which may provide the reader with the means of reducing his paperwork.

Getting people to talk to each other is not always easy, but it is made considerably worse by the way in which their workplaces are organized. Many executives like their own office where they can hide, often protected by an outer office manned by that formidable guardian known as the 'private secretary' or 'personal assistant'. These executives appear to deliberately make themselves difficult to talk to. The only method of approach is then the internal memo, which is often opened, and sometimes answered, by the secretary. These defences are not easy to break down and in the end people stop trying.

I believe that all such barriers should be broken down and that people should be available in either face to face situations or on the end of a telephone. Modern closed circuit television and telephone conference facilities are being increasingly used by forward thinking organizations. Unfortunately, many others have not even realized the merits of open-plan and landscaped offices.

The use of modern facilities (when they work) is a very important factor, but more important is the ability of people to talk to each other. The majority of businessmen are able to talk coherently, but very few can listen, and if people are going to talk to each other they are also going to have to listen.

I attended a meeting where three executives were intent upon agreeing a course of action for dealing with customers's complaints. Each had particularly strong views and appeared to be solely concerned with expressing them. They interposed their views preceded by comments such as 'That might work but', or 'I appreciate what you are saying, but'. Needless to say the meeting was unproductive. Afterwards I asked each in turn what suggestions had been made by the other executives. Without the minutes none could answer the question.

It might seem that only the secretary listens at meetings and that the persons attending read the minutes simply to ensure their own ideas were documented. This is, of course, an exaggerated view, but illustrates my point.

Some rules with respect to meetings:

1. Don't call a meeting if there is any other way of resolving the problem. If there's no problem, why call a meeting?
2. Don't go to meetings unless you can and ought to contribute
3. Scrap minutes and use action sheets (Fig. 10.2) clearly stating decisions made and action to be taken
4. Whenever a meeting is necessary ensure there is an agenda and that a time limit is set. I usually try to start a meeting at 11 a.m. with the aim of finishing at lunchtime
5. Try whenever possible to organize meetings in the morning when people are relatively fresh.

Whenever it is necessary to discuss a topic with someone, contact them to arrange a time and be sure they do the same with you. Nothing is more irritating or wasteful of time than 'popping in for a few words'. Such contact is rarely fruitful and often occurs because the person popping in has nothing better to do.

It is not always possible to talk direct even using modern technology. When this occurs paper is the fallback, but paper should only be used when all other methods have failed.

When it is necessary for several people to be involved in any project, ensure that a properly organized team or working party is established, definitely not a committee. In respect to committees remember that:

1. They are formed to obscure responsibility
2. The best committeeman is one who is incapable of making a decision on his own.

Committees can be useless when something has to be done quickly. They can be useful in obtaining different opinions, and in collecting information in a non-urgent situation. A sound project team requires a good leader, who must clearly define the purpose of the team, and its methods of operation. When the purpose of a team is achieved, disband it and move on to the next project. I would like to make two points in regard to organizing working parties.

1. It is often more difficult to follow than to lead
2. A good leader requires able and resourceful followers.

Progress Report

GROUP SYSTEMS PROJECT TEAM

DATE		NUMBER	

NARRATIVE	AMENDED DATES

Fig. 10.1   Progress report

When a project team has been formed it must, of course, meet from time to time to agree action and review progress. These meetings should only be held when necessary. If a good communications system is established, they will not have to be held frequently. I have found the following documents essential in running a project team.

1. A progress report (Fig. 10.1)
2. An action sheet (Fig. 10.2)
3. An information circular (Fig. 7.1, page 95).

The action sheet replaces the minutes of meetings and is perhaps one of the most important contributions I have made in reducing unnecessary paperwork.

Action Sheet

GROUP SYSTEMS PROJECT TEAM

MEETING NUMBER	AT	HELD ON

AGENDA	IN ATTENDANCE

DECISIONS

ACTION		
WHAT	WHO	WHEN

Fig. 10.2   Action sheet

The progress report is self-explanatory and should be used at either predetermined intervals or when there is something worth while to report.

The information circular bridges the gap between meetings and helps to keep everyone informed of the details of individual team members efforts.

The use of project teams, especially in the field of systems development, is highly recommended.

What can the individual paperworker do?

Every single person engaged in paperwork can help to reduce the alarming increase in useless pieces of paper. In my own view as much as 30 per cent of paperwork is composed of correspondence both internal and external, and in this area, the role of the individual is considerable. The following rules will help the reader to reduce paperwork.

1. Don't produce any if possible
2. When it is necessary to produce paperwork, ensure it is kept to a minimum
3. Don't keep copies unless it is absolutely necessary
4. Prefer a pen to a typewriter
5. When receiving paperwork, keep only what you need
6. Don't take unnecessary copies
7. Throw away as much paper as you can
8. Whenever you throw paper away check back to see where it came from to stop any more coming. Tell them you don't want it or that you throw it away; that usually works
9. Judge your success at paperwork control by the low level of paper going out of your office, and the lack of files you maintain.

Whenever you see your subordinates using methods which you consider wasteful, or acting in a way of which you disapprove, look carefully at your own methods and actions as they are almost certainly imitating you.

Conclusion

I have tried to ensure that the contents of this book are practical and of use to all paperworkers at all levels, particularly to those whose responsibility includes the review and design of systems.

The appendices contain considerable detail of how the procedures outlined in the book work in practice. I sincerely hope that you will find much you can use. In closing I would like to make a final point concerning waste.

A manager's opportunity to cause waste increases in proportion to his authority and status.

Appendices

Appendix 1
Procedure flowcharts

Flowcharts are an important tool in the pathfinder's kit. Without their use complex procedures become extremely difficult to decipher. The examples of the pathfinder's records (Appendix 2) indicate how clearly the procedure can be seen when a flowchart is prepared. In chapter 4 the use of the document and information flowchart was discussed and this form of flowchart is shown in Appendix 2.

The charting method I recommend is not the only method available. This appendix has been prepared to provide the reader with an indication of the alternatives.

The reasons for using charts are:

1. They force consideration of the procedure in a logical step by step sequence
2. They clearly indicate missing steps
3. They indicate deficiencies and duplication in the system
4. They eliminate the variable interpretation which can be placed on narrative procedures
5. They clearly show the path the procedures follow, on one piece of paper.

Flow chart symbols (in addition to those detailed in chapter 4)

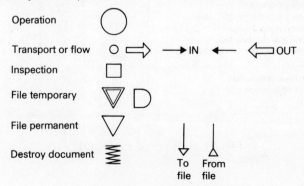

Operation

Transport or flow

Inspection

File temporary

File permanent

Destroy document

To file   From file

In order to illustrate the use of the charts contained in this appendix the following procedure will be charted on each example:

> Operator raises material requisition
> Stores issue goods
> Issue is recorded on the bin card
> Material requisition is coded and priced
> Material requisition is sent to the cost office
> Cost office sort and file material requisition.

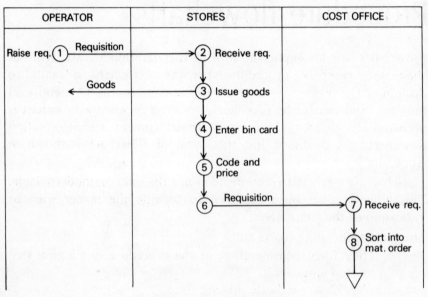

Fig. A1.1   Procedure chart (1)

LOCATION	OPERATION	MATERIAL REQUISITION	BIN CARD		
Workshop	Operator prepares requisition hands requisition to storeman				
Stores	Storeman receives requisition Issues materials Enters details on bin card Files bin card code and price requisition Send requisition to cost office				
Cost office	Receive requisition Sort requisition File				

Fig. A1.2   Procedure chart (2)

Procedure charts

Procedure charts as shown in Figs. A1.1 and A1.2 are an extension of the procedure narrative and the information flow records shown in Fig. 4.2 and Fig. 4.3, page 54 and 56. The addition of symbols and flow lines assists in determining the flow and the departmental interactions.

Process charts

Process charts as shown in Figs. A1.3 and A1.4 have been adapted from work-study techniques and are generally used during the investigation for the collection and classification of detailed operations. They are particularly useful in assessing work content in the office (see chapter 8, page 110).

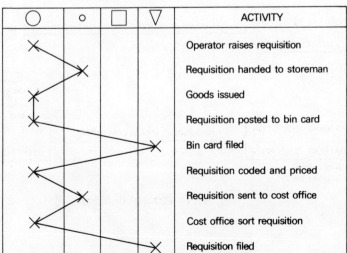

OPERATION	FLOW	CHECK	FILE	ACTIVITY
●	○	□	▽	Operator raises requisition
○	●	□	▽	Requisition handed to storeman
●	○	□	▽	Goods issued
●	○	□	▽	Requisition posted to bin card
○	○	□	▼	Bin card filed
●	○	□	▽	Requisition coded and priced
○	●	□	▽	Requisition sent to cost office
●	○	□	▽	Cost office sort requisition
○	○	□	▼	Requisition filed

Fig. A1.3 Process chart (1)

○	○	□	▽	ACTIVITY
×				Operator raises requisition
	×			Requisition handed to storeman
×				Goods issued
×				Requisition posted to bin card
			×	Bin card filed
×				Requisition coded and priced
	×			Requisition sent to cost office
×				Cost office sort requisition
			×	Requisition filed

137

Fig. A1.4   Process chart (2)

Flow process chart

This is a combination of the procedure chart and the process chart and provides a complete picture in respect of activities.

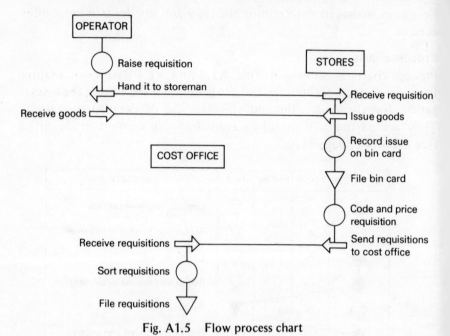

Fig. A1.5   Flow process chart

Pictorial flowchart

The pictorial flowchart, also called 'form flowchart', paints a picture of the documents and the entries, and gives an indication of the flow and the activities.

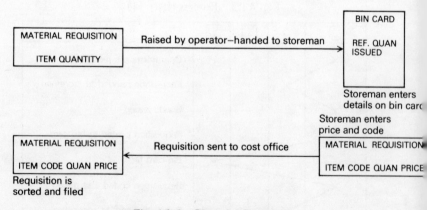

Fig. A1.6   Pictorial flowchart

Symbols

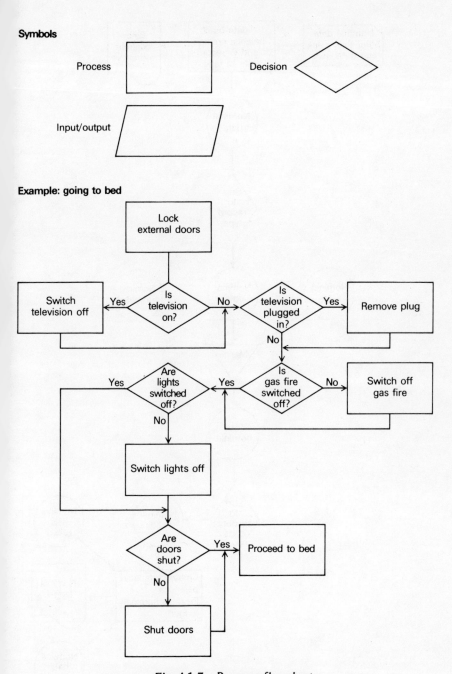

Process

Decision

Input/output

Example: going to bed

Fig. A1.7   Program flowchart

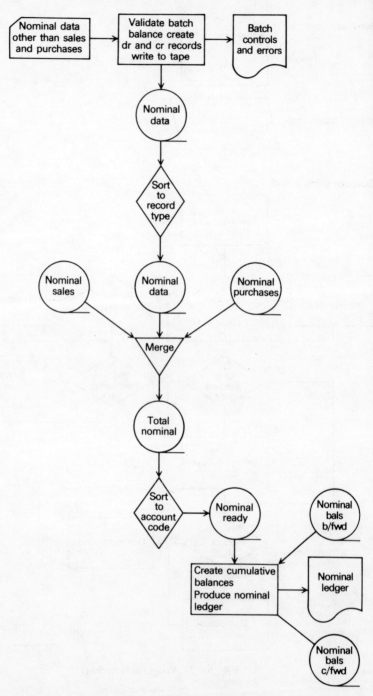

Fig. A1.8   Systems flowchart

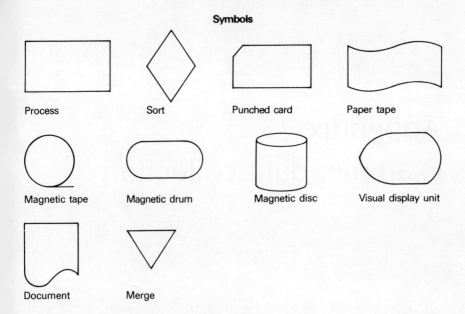

Symbols

Process   Sort   Punched card   Paper tape

Magnetic tape   Magnetic drum   Magnetic disc   Visual display unit

Document   Merge

Information and document flowchart

The information and document flowchart that I have developed combines the procedure/process/and pictorial charts, and provides a complete picture of the procedure and the forms used. See Appendix 2, Fig. A2.1, for an example of this type of chart.

Appendix 2
Example: data collection

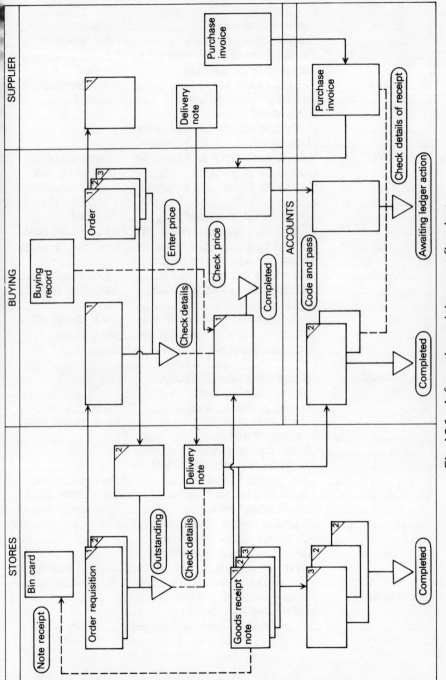

Fig. A2.1 Information and document flowchart

DEPARTMENT	ACTIVITY	DOCUMENT
Stores	Determine requirements	Bin card
	Request order	Order requisition
	File copy of request in outstanding file	" "
	Note request on bin card	Bin card
Buying	Receive request for order	Order requisition
	Obtain details of supplier	Buying record
	Place order	Order
	Distribute copy orders 1. Supplier	"
	File copy 3 2. Stores	"
Stores	Receive goods, check with copy order	Delivery note / order
	Note receipt of goods	Goods receipt note
	Distribute copies 1. Buying	" " "
	2. Accounts	" " "
	Enter details of receipt	Bin card
	File 3 copy of goods receipt note	Goods receipt note
	Extract copy order and order	Copy order / order req.
	requisition and file in the completed file	
Buying	Receive notification of receipt	Goods receipt note
	Extract outstanding file data	Copy order / order req.
	Check details	" "
	Enter price onto goods receipt note	Goods receipt note
	File copy orders in completed file	Copy order
	File goods receipt note in "awaiting	Goods receipt note
	invoice" file	
Accounts	Receive notification of receipt	"
	File in "awaiting invoice" file	"
	Receive purchase invoice	Purchase invoice
	Check purchase invoice with	Goods receipt note
	goods receipt note	
	Enter date received	"
	File goods receipt note in completed file	"
	Send invoice to Buying	Purchase Invoice
Buying	Check invoice with priced	Goods receipt note /
	goods receipt note	purchase invoice
	If price is correct sign invoice, if	"
	not correct query the invoice	"
	Settle query and pass invoice	"
	Enter new price on buying record	Buying record
	Send purchase invoices to accounts	Purchase invoice
Accounts	Receive purchase invoices	"
	Enter accounts codes	"
	File in "awaiting ledger posting" file	"

Fig. A2.2   Procedure narrative

PROCEDURE — Purchasing	Bin card	Order requisition	Official order	Buying record	Goods received note	Delivery note	Purchase invoice				Times entered
Item description	X	X	X		X	X	X				6
Item code	X	X	X		X	X	X				6
Minimum quantity	X										1
Maximum quantity	X										1
Re-order level	X										1
Re-order quantity	X	X	X	X	X	X	X				7
Bin location	X										1
Reference (goods rec. note)	X										1
Receipts	X										1
Issues	X										1
Suppliers name			X	X	X	X	X				5
Suppliers address			X			X	X				3
Order number			X	X	X	X	X				5
Order date			X	X							2
Price			X	X	X		X				4
Delivery period			X	X							2
Company's name			X			X	X				3
Company's address			X			X	X				3
Delivery point			X			X	X				3
Conditions of purchase			X								1
Invoice address			X				X				2
Delivery note number					X	X	X				3
Value					X		X				2
Invoice number							X				1
Order requisition date		X									1
Delivery note date					X	X	X				3
Invoice date							X				1

Fig. A2.3   X chart

FORM TITLE	Bin card		SOURCE	Stores
PURPOSE	To record transactions for each item held in stock			
COPIES	DISTRIBUTION		PURPOSE	
1	Held in stores		As above	

DEPARTMENT	DATA ENTERED	DATA EXTRACTED
Stores	Item description	Balance — Stock taking
	Item code number	Item description
	Bin location	Item code
	Reference	Re-order quantity
	Receipts	
	Issues	
	Balance	
	Minimum quantity	
	Maximum quantity	
	Re-order level	
	Re-order quantity	

DATA CARRIED
See 'data entered'

TIMING

PLACE WHERE FORM FILED	REFERRED TO BY:	PERIOD FORM RETAINED	VOLUME PER MONTH
Stores	Storeman	Completed cards held for 12 months	20 new items

Fig. A2.4   Form detail sheet—bin card

FORM TITLE	Buying record		SOURCE	Buying
PURPOSE	To provide a history of dealings with each supplier			
COPIES	DISTRIBUTION		PURPOSE	
1	Buying department		As above	

DEPARTMENT	DATA ENTERED	DATA EXTRACTED
Buying	Item description	Suppliers name
	Item code	Price
	Suppliers name	Delivery period
	Order number	
	Date	
	Quantity ordered	
	Price	
	Delivery period	
	Re-order level	

DATA CARRIED

TIMING

PLACE WHERE FORM FILED	REFERRED TO BY:	PERIOD FORM RETAINED	VOLUME PER MONTH
Buying	Order clerk	Indefinitely	20 new items

Fig. A2.5   Form detail sheet—buying record

FORM TITLE	Order requisition		SOURCE	Stores
PURPOSE	To initiate an official order from buying department			
COPIES	DISTRIBUTION		PURPOSE	
1	Buying department		To initiate order	
2	Stores		Record of request for an order	

DEPARTMENT	DATA ENTERED	DATA EXTRACTED
Stores	Date Item description Item code Quantity required	
Buying		Item description Item code Quantity

DATA CARRIED

TIMING

PLACE WHERE FORM FILED	REFERRED TO BY:	PERIOD FORM RETAINED	VOLUME PER MONTH
Stores	Stores clerk	2 years	
Buying	Order clerk	Indefinitely	200

Fig. A2.6   Form detail sheet—order requisition

FORM TITLE	Official order		SOURCE	Buying
PURPOSE	To obtain supplies from the supplier			
COPIES	DISTRIBUTION		PURPOSE	
1	Supplier		To obtain supplies	
2	Stores		Notification of source of supply	
3	Buying		Record	

DEPARTMENT	DATA ENTERED	DATA EXTRACTED
Buying	Suppliers name and address	
	Item description	
	Item reference	
	Price	
	Quantity	
	Delivery period	

DATA CARRIED

Company's name and address ⎱
Delivery point
Conditions of purchase ⎬ Preprinted
Order number
Invoice address ⎰

TIMING

PLACE WHERE FORM FILED	REFERRED TO BY:	PERIOD FORM RETAINED	VOLUME PER MONTH
Buying	Order clerk	Indefinitely	
Stores	Stores clerk	12 months	280

Fig. A2.7   Form detail sheet—official order

FORM TITLE	Purchase invoice		SOURCE	Supplier
PURPOSE	To obtain payment			
COPIES	DISTRIBUTION		PURPOSE	
1	Accounts department		Payment of supplier	

DEPARTMENT	DATA ENTERED	DATA EXTRACTED
Accounts	Date goods received Invoice number (internal) Accounts code	Suppliers invoice No. Value

DATA CARRIED

Suppliers name and address Value
Order number reference Date
Suppliers invoice number Delivery note needed
Item description
Item code
Price

TIMING

PLACE WHERE FORM FILED	REFERRED TO BY:	PERIOD FORM RETAINED	VOLUME PER MONTH
Accounts	Purchase invoice clerk Accountant Purchase ledger clerk	Indefinitely	250

Fig. A2.8 Form detail sheet—purchase invoice

FORM TITLE	Delivery note		SOURCE	Supplier
PURPOSE	Record of goods despatched			
COPIES	DISTRIBUTION		PURPOSE	
1	Stores		As above	

DEPARTMENT	DATA ENTERED	DATA EXTRACTED
Stores		Delivery note number
		Quantity received

DATA CARRIED

Suppliers name and address
Delivery note number
Quantity
Item description
Item code number
Date   Order number

TIMING

PLACE WHERE FORM FILED	REFERRED TO BY:	PERIOD FORM RETAINED	VOLUME PER MONTH
Stores	Stores clerk	12 months	300

Fig. A2.9   Form detail sheet—delivery note

FORM TITLE	Goods received note		SOURCE	Stores
PURPOSE	To notify departments concerned of receipt of goods			
COPIES	DISTRIBUTION		PURPOSE	
1	Buying	} As above		
2	Accounts			
3	Stores	Record		

DEPARTMENT	DATA ENTERED	DATA EXTRACTED
Stores	Suppliers name Date Order number Item description	
	Item code Quantity Delivery note number	
Buying	Price	
Accounts	Price Value	

DATA CARRIED

TIMING

PLACE WHERE FORM FILED	REFERRED TO BY:	PERIOD FORM RETAINED	VOLUME PER MONTH
Buying	Order clerk	} Indefinitely	
Accounts	Purchase invoice clerk		300
Stores	Stores clerk	12 months	

Fig. A2.10   Form detail sheet—goods received note

DEPARTMENT	INDIVIDUAL	ACTIVITY	FORMS USED	FILES USED	RECORDS USED	OTHER INFORMATION USED	SOURCE
Accounts	Purchase invoice clerk	Receive goods rec. note	Goods rec. note	Outstanding file			
		Check purchase invoice	Purchase invoice, Goods rec. note	—"—			
		Coding and passing Purchase invoice	Code list			Knowledge of analysis of purchases	Accountant
		Filing invoices		File "Awaiting ledger action"			

Fig. A2.11   Activity schedule—accounts

153

DEPARTMENT	Buying						
INDIVIDUAL	ACTIVITY	FORMS USED	FILES USED	RECORDS USED	OTHER INFORMATION USED	SOURCE
Order clerk	Receive orders	Official order		Buying record		
	Maintain records	Order requisition		Buying record		
	Completion of order	goods received note	Outstanding file			
	Check price of invoice	Purchase invoice	Completed file			
Buyer	Sign and vet order	Official order				

Fig. A2.12   Activity schedule—buying

DEPARTMENT	Stores						
INDIVIDUAL	ACTIVITY	FORMS USED	FILES USED	RECORDS USED	OTHER INFORMATION USED	SOURCE	
Stores record clerk	Prepare order reqs.	Order requisition					
	Maintain records		Outstanding file				
	Receive goods	Delivery note					
	Prepare goods receipt note	Goods receipt note	Completed file				
Storeman	Assessing requirements	Bin card					
	Receive goods						

Fig. A2.13 Activity schedule—stores

155

Appendix 3
Example of analysis and specification

Analysis

Using the example in Appendix 2 the steps of the analysis process, namely:

1. Key activities
2. Secondary activities
3. Unnecessary activities
4. Poor workflow
5. Surplus documents
6. Duplication of effort
7. Unnecessary information

have been carried out and the following notes summarize the findings.

Key activities:
    (a) Buying the goods
    (b) Receiving the goods
    (c) Paying for the goods.

Secondary activities:
    (a) Maintaining buying records
    (b) Maintaining stores records
    (c) Notifying accounts of transactions.

Unnecessary activities:

    (a) Filing of goods receipt notes in three places
    (b) Checking details of receipt three times.

Poor workflow:

> The flow of work between stores and buying, and between buying and accounts is cumbersome with several documents being handled more than once.

Surplus documents:

(a) Question the need for an order requisition
(b) Question the need for three copies of the goods receipt note.

Duplication of effort:

> Filing and checking as noted under unnecessary activities.

Unnecessary information:

> Reference to the X chart (Fig. A2.3) indicates several pieces of information which are recorded on more than one document. Question the purpose for this and assess the minimum data required.

Establishing the problem

In this example it is apparent that the system is at fault, and that there are too many activities and too much paperwork. It would seem appropriate to design revised procedures to overcome these problems. A slight change of responsibility may be needed to smooth the flow of information.

Developing alternative solutions

Referring to the analysis of the existing procedure it is obvious that any alternative must

1. Improve the workflow
2. Eliminate filing and checking activities
3. Reduce the number of documents
4. Reduce the amount of information being handled.

Several solutions present themselves when the following questions have been asked in reference to the present procedure:

> How else?
> Where else?
> What else?
> When else?
> Who else?

The alternative solutions for consideration are as follows:

1. Allow stores to place orders and to pass invoices for payment This will eliminate several documents and activities, and a good deal of information flow
2. Reduce the paperwork by the introduction of a travelling bin card
3. Combine certain operations in the accounts and buying, so that the accounts can pass the invoice without reference to the buying
4. Use the supplier's delivery note in place of the goods receipt note
5. A combined approach covering the points outlined in alternatives 2, 3, and 4.

In order to assess these alternatives, they are checked against the system specification in general to see if they are valid solutions. From the checklist on the systems specification it is apparent that alternative 1 is not valid, but that the remainder are.

The next task of selecting the most appropriate alternative is carried out by drawing flowcharts for each alternative, and then discussing these in principle with management. When the views of the people concerned have been gathered the selection of the solution should be straightforward.

TITLE	Buying and receipt of goods	ALTERNATIVES							
		1	2	3	4	5	6	7	8
PURPOSE	To purchase stores requirements and to ensure goods are paid for.	?	√	√	√	√			
REQUIREMENTS	1. Official order for all purchases	√	√	√	√	√			
	2. Buying record	√	√	√	√	√			
	3. Record of receipts	√	√	√	√	√			
	4. Notification of receipts to accounts	?	√	√	√	√			
	5. Passing suppliers invoice for payment	√	√	√	√	√			
CONSTRAINTS	1. Stores personnel are not to purchase direct	X	√	√	√	√			
	2. Accounts are responsible for passing invoices for payment	X	√	√	√	√			
	3. Buyer must verify prices	X	√	√	√	√			
SOLUTIONS	Stores ordering and invoice checking (present system)	1							
	Travelling bin card		2						
	Accounts using copy order			3					
	Use of suppliers delivery note				4				
	Combined approach of 2. 3. 4					5			
							6		
								7	
									8

Fig. A3.1   System specification

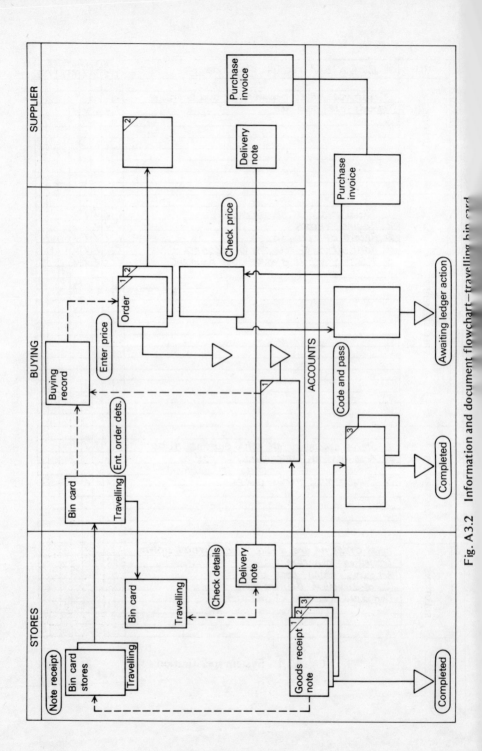

Fig. A3.2   Information and document flowchart—travelling bin card

160

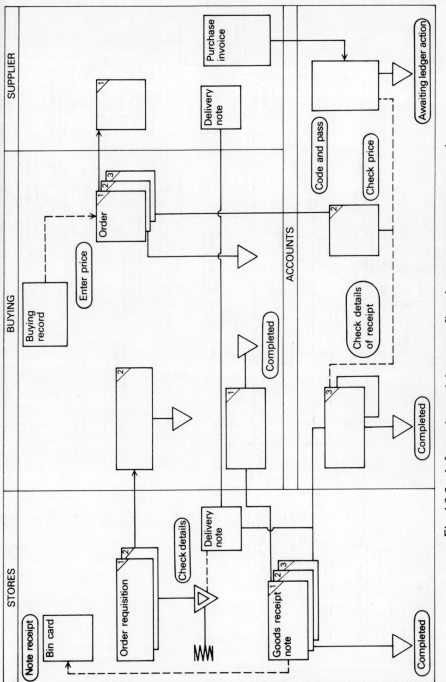

Fig. A3.3   Information and document flowchart—accounts use copy order

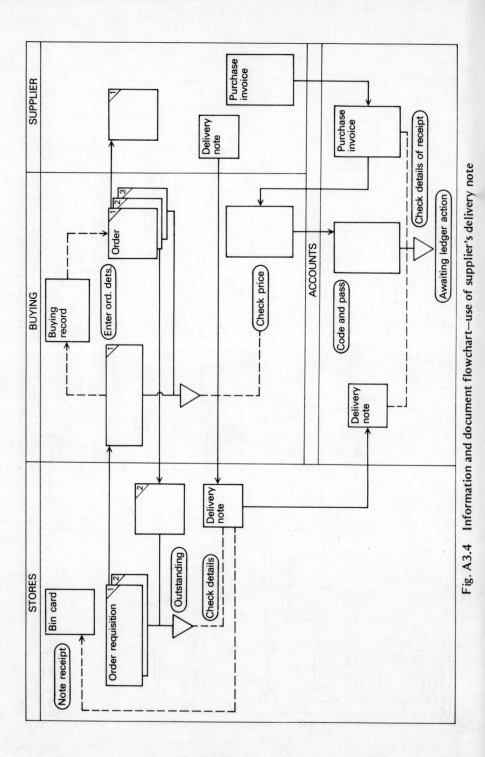

Fig. A3.4 Information and document flowchart—use of supplier's delivery note

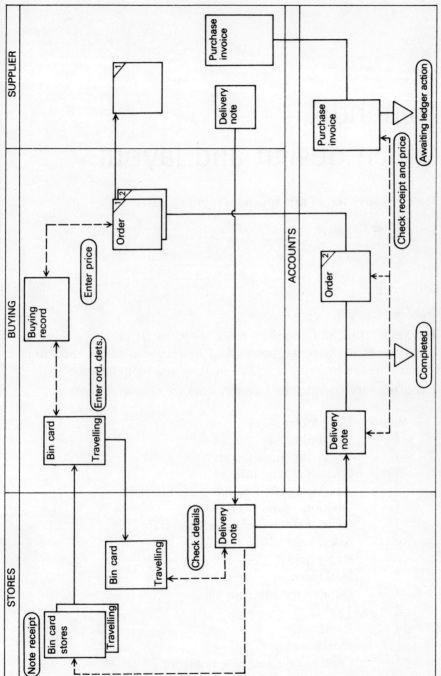

Fig. A3.5   Information and document flowchart—combined approach

163

Appendix 4
Office design and layout

The example given in this appendix is in two parts:

Office design
Layout

Office design

Problem:

The head office of a company has decided to set up a new factory. The systems designer has been asked to design an office, indicating the area needed in terms of square meters for a room height of 3 m.

The offices are intended to accommodate the following staff:

Number	Description
1	Local director
1	Local director's secretary
1	Divisional accountant
7	Accounts staff (including a/c machine)
1	Divisional sales manager
1	Divisional sales manager's secretary
10	Sales/order office staff
1	Receptionist
1	Mail room
1	Duplicating and copying
2	Typing
1	Filing
1	Works manager
1	Canteen (vending machines) for office and works
1	Conference room.

The Board of Directors have decided to attach the office to the works as a single storey extension.

The factory will employ between 100 and 150.

An information room is considered desirable for drawings and specifications.

Considerations

1. Define the purpose of the office:
   In this case the purpose of the office is to meet the administrative needs of the factory.

2. Establish limiting factors:
   Single storey office 3 m high. Windows on three sides.

3. Determine occupants of the office:
   As listed.

4. Status limits:
   These apply to the:

   > Local Director
   > Divisional Sales Manager
   > Divisional Accountant.

5. Equipment requirements:
   Accounting machine and vending machines and service equipment, i.e., typing, duplicating, copying, etc.

6. Services required.

7. Requirements of Offices Act:
   400 cubic feet (11.2 m^3) per person.

8. Departmental relationships:
   > Sales order office and Div. Sales Manager
   > Accounts and Div. Accountant
   > Local Director and Senior Managers
   > Works Manager and Works
   > Cloakrooms and Canteen.

9. Security.

10. Movement in the offices:
    By considering relationships and the design of corridors, etc.

11. Levels of noise:
    Curtailed by keeping equipment out of general offices as far as possible.

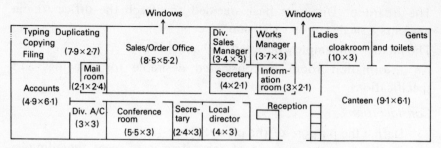

Fig. A4.1   Solution to office layout problem

Office layout

Problem

The accounts office in the new office building must be laid out to cater for the equipment and workflow needs shown on page 167.

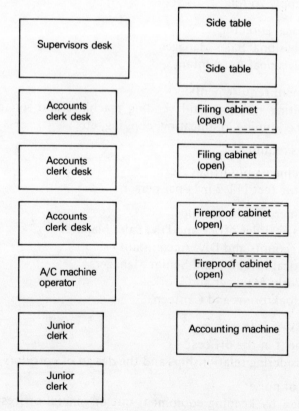

Fig. A4.2   Desks and equipment

Staff	Equipment
Supervisor	Desk. 150 cm x 100 cm
A/c machine operator	Desk. 140 cm x 80 cm
3 accounts clerks	3 Desks. 140 cm x 80 cm.
	2 Side Tables. 140 cm x 50 cm
2 junior clerks	2 Desks. 120 cm x 60 cm
	1 Accounting Machine. 150 cm x 80 cm
	2 Fireproof filing cabinets
	(open). 150 cm x 60 cm
	1 Ordinary filing cabinet
	(open). 140 cm x 50 cm.

In addition, the room must be laid out for an efficient workflow in that the juniors assist the accounting machine operator by 'pulling' and 'stuffing' in the ledger trays filed in the fireproof cabinets.

The supervisor does accounting machine work when necessary.

The work of the three accounts clerks is related.

The supervisor requires use of internal and external phone.

The a/c machine operation requires use of internal and external phone.

The accounts clerks each require use of internal and external phones.

Apart from the juniors, all other staff must be near to power points for adding machines and calculators.

Considerations

1. Space available (6 m x 5 m)
2. Location of equipment
3. Workflow in the office
4. Lighting, etc.

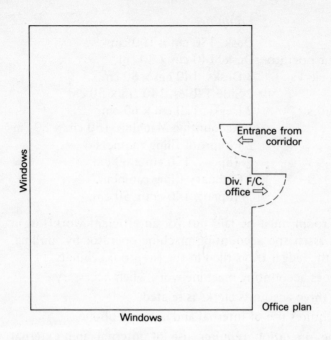

Office plan

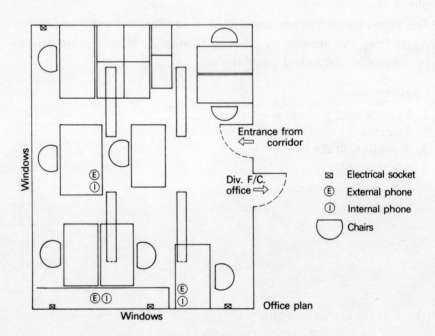

⊠	Electrical socket
Ⓔ	External phone
Ⓘ	Internal phone
⌒	Chairs

Office plan

Fig. A4.3

Appendix 5
Assessing work content

Before it is possible to measure the time it should take to do a particular job, it is essential to break that job down into a series of elements which cover the work content. It is far more important to know the work content than to know how long it takes to complete the task. In the process of assessing work content it frequently happens that unnecessary steps can be eliminated.

There are several ways of assessing work content. The one I have outlined here has provided considerable benefits, and in only a few cases where it has been applied has it been considered necessary to extend the analysis into detailed work measurement.

Stage 1 Work content assessment form (Fig. A5.1)
The prime function of this form is to break down the activity into a number of elements, which can be analysed in detail as to:
1. Paperwork used
2. Type of work
3. Volume of work
4. Level of work

> RND   Routine non-discretionary
> RD   Routine discretionary
> NRND Non-routine—non-discretionary
> NRD   Non-routine—discretionary.

The example shown covers an activity concerned with pricing and coding delivery notes for invoicing and analysis, both for an existing system and a planned system.

Stage 2 Workflow relationships (Fig. A5.2)
This form is used to show the relationship of the activity being assessed with other activities, by determining the data inputs and outputs of the activity.

DEPARTMENT	Nth. Yorks – Sales		ACTIVITY	Pricing and coding

ELEMENT OF WORK	DOCUMENT	VOLUME	FREQ.	SOURCE	READ	WRITE	SORT	COLLATE	FILE	RETRIEVE	BATCH	TOTAL	CALCULATE	CHECK	KEY	CHARACTERS	MANUAL	MACHINE	TYPE OF MACHINE	R.N.D	R.D	N.R.D	N.R.D	GENERAL
Receive delivery note	Delivery note	3000	D	Depots	✓									✓		4		✓	Adding	✓				
Refer to price file	Price card	750	D	Pricing	✓					✓						25	✓				✓			
Enter details	Summary sheet	600	D	Depots		✓										25	✓				✓			
Filing price card	Price card	100	D	Quote office				✓								1	✓				✓			
	Summary sheets	600	D	Depots							✓	✓				—	✓	✓	Adding		✓			
Batch	Batch slip	10	D	Pricing	✓											20	✓				✓			
NEW PROCEDURE																								
Receive summary sheets	Summary sheets	600	D	Depots	✓									✓		4		✓	Adding		✓			
Refer to price file	Price card	100	D	Pricing	✓					✓						6	✓				✓			
Enter reg. code	Summary sheet	600	D	Depots		✓										6	✓				✓			
Filing price card	Price card	100	D	Quote office				✓								1	✓				✓			
Terminal input	Summary sheet	600	D	Depots	✓										✓	19		✓	Computer terminal				✓	

Fig. A5.1   Work content assessment form

| DEPARTMENT | NTH. YORKS–SALES | ACTIVITY | PRICING and CODING |

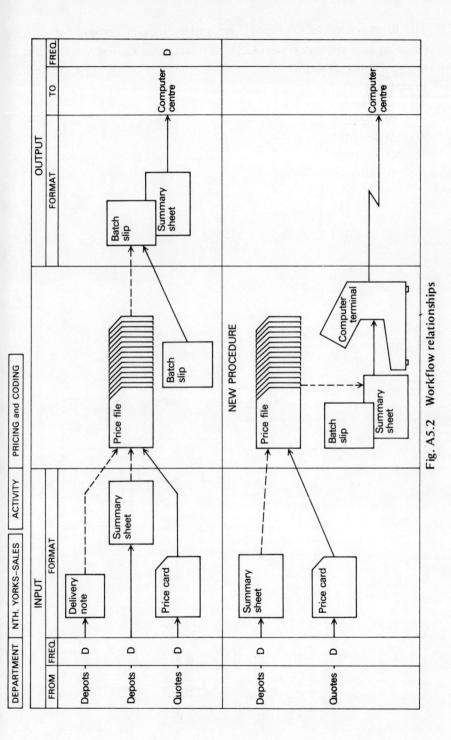

Fig. A5.2 Workflow relationships

The form is used as a flowchart with narrative descriptions.

Once again, the example used relates to an existing system and a proposed new system.

Frequency
- D Daily
- W Weekly
- M Monthly
- Q Quarterly
- A Annually.

Appendix 6
Forms control

1. The case for central forms control

1.1 Business forms are the basis of most if not all systems, and if they are not carefully controlled in terms of design, make-up and appearance can seriously damage the effectiveness of any system. There are three areas in which control can yield considerable benefits

      1.1.1. Consistency of data
      1.1.2. Efficiency of clerical effort
      1.1.3. Economy of supply

2. Consistency of data

2.1 Local needs for forms if answered without consideration to the communication of information in a common understandable format can lead to misunderstanding and inefficiency.

2.2 Such local forms use often leads to unofficial and often unintentional systems changes, which can seriously impair the results of the system.

2.3 Terminology differs within an organization, and a standard form will prevent many problems, e.g.

Date
Despatch date   can all be used to
Delivery date   mean the same thing
Date goods sent

3. Efficiency of clerical effort

3.1 The non-conformity of forms with different terminology can lead to wasted time in identifying the information and making records or producing input.

3.2 Carefully designed forms with the use of colours and identification of distribution will go a long way towards eliminating many small, frustrating inefficiencies.

4. Economy of supply

4.1 Concentration of purchasing potential is achieved by three means:

   4.1.1. Central buying
   4.1.2. Central storing
   4.1.3. Avoidance of inessential variety.

4.2 By obtaining all supplies from a smaller number of suppliers, volume is increased and terms become more favourable, as does the price in that 10 000 forms cost less than 10 x 1000 when printed separately.

4.3 Central buying and central storage go hand in hand in order to obtain the advantages in 4.2.

4.4 Central forms design in reducing the variety of forms will increase the volumes of common forms and produce savings. That is not to say that all forms can be made common, but that those that can should be.

4.5 Designing for economic print production, and therefore lower cost, requires a certain expertise and an understanding of paper sizes and printing processes available. The rewards, however, can be considerable.

5. Features of central forms control

5.1 Common design disciplines are required to facilitate the designing of specific forms to consistent design standards.

5.2 A forms identification system and a comprehensive form library with up to date samples.

5.3 Provision of a forms design service in response to requests from management, which enables the forms use and its effects on the overall management information system to be assessed.

5.4 A central store for common stationery supplies and procedures for purchasing and requisitioning of supplies.

5.5 Careful control of all sequentially renumbered forms and a monitoring of print quality and price.

6. The controlling system

6.1 Form identification and a form library are the two essential features of form control, together with a form specification and record card used for printing and costing.

6.2 Form identification is achieved by using a title and a unique reference number. The reference number should incorporate a prefix or suffix identifying the user department. Forms used by more than one department should have no prefix or suffix.

6.3 A form library consisting of a copy of the form specification and the latest sample of the form, filed sequentially is an essential feature for the control of amendments and the checking of user requirements, i.e., is what has been ordered the same as the sample? Artwork and plates would be filed separately in parallel in the print room.

6.4 In addition to the form library, an index of all forms should be maintained on a strip index system both numerically and alphabetically (to avoid duplicating titles).

6.5 The form specification and record card covers the following:
    6.5.1. The form make-up for printing purposes.
    6.5.2. Initial record of cost (which becomes the standard).
    6.5.3. Record of supplies of the form.
    6.5.4. Whether printed or purchased outside; if purchased outside, where from and at what price.

6.6 To summarize the following records are required:
    6.6.1. Strip index—numerical, for issuing numbers and reference.
    6.6.2. Strip index—alphabetical, for issuing titles and reference.
    6.6.3. Form specification and record card (see sample).
    6.6.4. Form library (the copy of the spec. with a sample of the form).
    6.6.5. Artwork and plate library.

STATIONERY REQUISITION

FROM: NAME:
DIVISION:
DEPOT/OFFICE

DATE	DESCRIPTION	REF.	QUANTITY

SPECIAL REMARKS:

PRINTING DEPARTMENT USE ONLY

DESPATCH DETAILS

DATE	METHOD	No. OF PARCELS

COST	LABOUR	MATERIALS	EXTERNAL	O'HDS	TOTAL

JOB DETAILS:

PLEASE ENCLOSE SAMPLES

STATIONERY DELIVERY NOTE

FROM: NAME:
DIVISION:
DEPOT/OFFICE

DATE	DESCRIPTION	REF.	QUANTITY

SPECIAL REMARKS:

DESPATCH DETAILS

DATE	METHOD	No. OF PARCELS

Fig. A6.1 Stationery requisition

Form Specification and Record Card

FORM:

FORM NUMBER

FORM TITLE

FORM HISTORY

DETAILS			FORM CONTROL	VALUE					PRINT ROOM	
DATE	DATE REQUIRED	AMEND'MT	DATE PASSED	QUANTITY	LABOUR	MATS	EXTERNAL	O'HD	TOTAL	DATE COMPILED	PRE-NUMBERING, ETC.

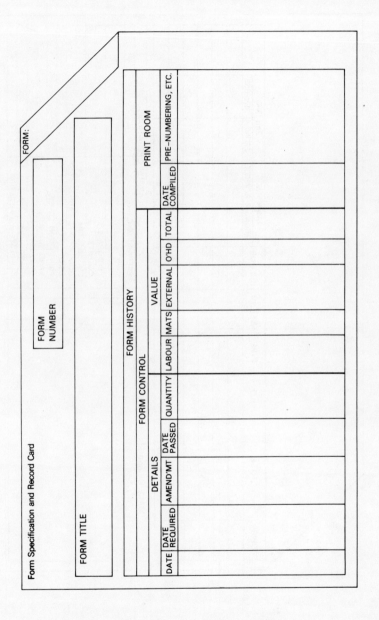

COPIES	TITLE	SIZE	TYPE	WEIGHT	COLOUR	MAIN INK		2nd INK	
						FRONT	REVERSE	FRONT	REVERSE

MAKE UP and SPECIAL INSTRUCTIONS

LABOUR OPERATIONS

PREPARE MACHINE
PRINT
PUNCH
PERFORATE
COLLATE
CUT and TRIM
GUMUP—SETS—PADS
BIND
PRINT FRONT COVER
HAND NUMBER
MAKE UP
STAPLE
FILE PLATE and ARTWORK

Fig. A6.2

6.7 In addition, a file of requisitions by division will enable the workflow, i.e., outstanding and completed work, to be controlled.

7. Using the service

7.1 From the management's point of view the operation of form control must be simple and routine. To effect this, a simple two-part form is all that is required.

7.2 Stationery requisition (Fig. A6.1) has two copies, both of which are sent to form control. The top copy acts as a delivery note and is released with the supply of forms. The second copy acts as a cost record, etc., and is used in form control.

8. Conclusion

8.1 The importance of forms control is not generally appreciated. The effect of exercising control as indicated above, can produce considerable savings.

8.2 In one recent exercise I carried out the number of forms in use was reduced by over 50 per cent and a saving of £4 000 per annum was achieved.

8.3 A final warning note, the aim of form control is to reduce both the number and cost of forms and not to create a self-perpetuating and increasingly costly reprographic department.

Bibliography

Organization & Methods, G. E. Milward, Macmillan, 1967.
Handbook of O & M Analysis, W. A. R. Webster, Business Books, 1973.
Up The Organisation, Robert Townsend, Coronet, 1970.
Analysing and Controlling Business Procedures, John O'Shaughnessy, Cassell, 1970.
O & M International Conference Proceedings, 1975.
'Designing an Information System that meets the Needs of Management', T. J. Bentley, *Management Accounting*, Nov. 1974.
Look Behind You, David Moreau, Associated Business Programmes, 1973.
The Accountant and Computers, A. J. Thomas, Pitman, 1967.
Basic Digital Computer Concepts, D. Whitworth, Heinemann, 1965.
The Effective use of Computers in Business, P. A. Losty, Cassell, 1969.
Introducing Computers, Murray Laver, HMSO, 1973.
The Computer Revolution, E. A. Thomeski, Macmillan, 1970.
Accounting and Computer Systems, H. D. Clifton and T. Lucey, Business Books, 1973.
The Art of Systems Analysis, B. Byrne, A. Mullally and D. Rothery, Business Books, 1969.
The Effective Computer, K. Grindley and J. Humble, McGraw-Hill, 1973.
Manual of Cost Reduction Techniques, Magnus Radke, McGraw-Hill, 1972.
'Too Much Management, Too Little Change', L. B. Moore, *Harvard Business Review*, Jan/Feb, 1956.
Modern Organisational Theory, C. Argyris, Wiley, 1959.
Industrial Work Groups, L. Sayles, Wiley, 1959.
Making Changes, A. S. Judson, Wiley, 1959.
Design of Forms in Government Departments, HMSO, 1972.
Modern Filing Methods and Equipment, G. Continolo, Business Books, 1970.
Multiple-part Business Forms, E. Lennox Muir, Cassell, 1971.
Documentation, Frank Whitehouse, Business Books, 1971.
Effective presentation, Anthony Jay, BIM, 1973.
Business Equipment Guide, BED Business Books (published annually).

Index

Accuracy, 20, 113
Action sheet, 127, 129
Activity schedules, 38, 153-5
Administration, 33
Alternatives, 68, 157
Analysis, 60-1, 156
Assignment brief, 46
Audio typing, 23
Auditors, 20

Book worm, 17

Centralize, 74
Change, 94
    effects of, 96
    initiated, 93
    introduction of, 92
    planning for, 102
    problems of, 96
    reactions to, 100
    reactive, 92
    resistance to, 100
Charts, 61, 81
Checker, 20
Checking, 20-1
Classification, 117
Clerical activities, 59
Clerk, 24
Coding, 117
Collecting data, 34, 142
Collecting information, 50
Committees, 127
Commonsense, 124
Communications, 4, 6, 8, 28, 101, 116, 125, 129
Compulsion, 101
Computers, 7, 117
Consistency, 173
Controls, 117
Conversion, 22, 122
Converter, 22
Coordination, 9

Copier, 17
Correspondence, 17-18
Creativity, 71

Data processing, 12
Data transmission, 74
Decentralize, 74
Demonstration, 81
Desks, 109
Destroyer, 26
Diagrams, 81
Dictating machine, 23
Discussion, 80
Documentation, 50
Documents, surplus, 62
Duplication, 62

Economy, 174
Environment, 66, 74, 107, 117
Equipment filing, 12
    office requirements, 111
    specification, 89
    selection of, 88
Errors, 20-1, 114, 115
    causes, 115
    correction, 123
Example, setting the right, 119

Face to face, 18, 116, 125
Faults, management, 115
Faults in methods, 116
Filer, 25
Filing, 121
    equipment, 12
    systems, 11, 25
Flexible hours, 120
Flowcharts, 57, 72, 77, 113, 135-9
    information and documentation, 62, 141, 143, 160-3
    pictorial, 138
    procedure, 136-7

Flowcharts—contd.
  program, 139
  symbols, 135, 141
  systems, 140
Followers, 128
Forms, purpose of, 35
  control, 173
Form design, 83
Form detail sheet, 35, 146-52
Form identification, 175
Form library, 175
Fountain of knowledge, 28

Grapevine, 28

How?, 51, 72
Human problems, 96

Ideas, 57
Implementation, 91
Information, 3, 7, 30, 46
  circular, 95, 130
  flow, 55
Initiated change, 93
Insecurity, 98
Introducing change, 92
Introducing systems, 91
Internal memo, 16
Interviewing, 40

Key activities, 61, 72

Leader, 128
Legibility, 114
Listen, 127
Location, 74

Machines, 22
Management, 7, 92, 119
  agreement, 76-7, 81
  involvement, 73, 90
Meetings, 127
  formal, 80
  rules, 127
Methods, 72
Microfilm, 25

Natural break, 74
New system, 90

Objects, 48
Objectivity, 50, 61, 74

Office, 5, 107
  conditions, 107
  design, 107, 164
  layout, 107-8, 166
Offices, Shops and Railway Premises
  Act 1963, 109
opinion, 65

Paper, 3
  carrier, 29
  creator, 16
Paperwork, 5
  control of, 33
Paperworker, 15, 130
Participation, 102
Paths, 45, 49
Pathfinder, 44
Peaks, 76
Persuasion, 101
Photocopy, 17
Presentation, 81
Privileges, 119
Problems, 71
  identification of, 64, 157
Procedure flowchart, 55, 136-7
  manual, 49
  narrative, 54, 144
Processing, 12
Project leader, 128
Project team, 128
Progress report, 130
Punch operator, 24

Quality, 123
Quality control, 113
Questions, 50, 63, 68, 71, 101-3, 157
Questions, sequence of, 39

Reactive change, 92
Reader, 18
Recording, 11, 54
Redundancy, 101
Reports, 77, 124
  format, 78
  preparation of, 78
  numbering, 79
  use of, 77
Resistance to change, 82
Respect, 119
Retrieval, 11, 26
Reviewing, 69

Sampling, 20
Secondary activities, 62

Secretary, 126
Selling ideas, 77
Shorthand, 23
Solutions, 69, 71, 157
Staffing levels, 75, 76
Systems, design of, 71
    designer, 71
    origin of, 34
    new, 90
    requirements, 71
    specification, 63, 66-7, 159
Symbols, 58, 135, 141

Talk, 126
Telex, 29
Terminal, 25
The Calf Path, 43
Time keeping, 119
Timing, 76, 102, 115, 123
Trust, 99, 119
    lack of, 33

Typewriters, 122
Typing, 122

Unnecessary activities, 62

Visual aids, 81

Waste, 131
What?, 50
When?, 51, 72
Where?, 51, 76
Who?, 38, 51, 75
Why?, 53
Work content, 110, 169
    assessment form, 170
Workflow, 111
    relationships, 169, 171
Work measurement, 110, 169
Work places, 126

X chart, 59, 145

Printed by William Clowes & Sons Ltd., London, Colchester and Beccles